7STEPUX®

The complete UX process from strategy to design

By Csaba Házi

7STEPUX®

The complete UX process from strategy to design

By Csaba Házi

Contents

Special thanks to Dániel Knaust, Dávid Dorosz, Emilio Barajas, Ferenc Fodor, and Zsuzsa Pongrácz for helping me write and publish this book.

Preface

Actually, I didn't want to write a book. Originally, I wrote a bunch of how-to guides for my team back when I was running my UX agency. There are lots of methods and frameworks to follow when it comes to the world of UX, and an enormous number of articles, podcasts, and books are available on the subject. Despite all the materials out there, I've heard from a lot of people that it's difficult to understand UX and that it's also difficult to see through the whole product development process.

You can read many great books that focus on different aspects of UX, and later on, I'll recommend a couple of books to help you get started. However, most of the books aren't practical enough. I love to teach others and act as a mentor. Over and over again, I would tell UX beginners to sit down and read *Lean UX, Don't Make Me Think,* or any other "standard" book out there on the market. Although they're all excellent books, after reading them, most of my apprentices still asked me, "How do I get started? What are the steps that I need to follow? What comes next?"

Blogs are another great source of knowledge. To be honest, there's a great deal that can be learned from good UX blogs. So, what's the point of this book? Well, a blog post can be very practical. For example, it can tell you how to use a wireframing tool step by step. But, you have to find relevant blogs and dig deep to find articles that aren't vague or tailored exclusively for the big companies. Obviously, this search process takes some time.

So, with this book, I want to ensure that you have a hands-on, practical UX guide that will give you an overview of how a UX process works and that's practical enough to get you started.

Let's be clear on one thing: My goal was not to write a thousand-page-long, jargon-ridden, unfeasible, overly professional guide. Instead, here's what you can expect from this book:

- You can expect to see the steps that ensure a good UX process.
- You can expect a breakdown for each step so that you can see what methods can be applied.
- You can expect to learn and understand what those methods are good for and how to use them.

The last point is extremely important. Believe it or not, this book has been written, drafted, and carefully created by following this UX process. Well, sort of... I tested every chapter with multiple reviewers to get the most out of it. I asked them to answer the following questions after they read about each phase/stage:

- What is it about? What does that method or technique do?
- Why is that method or technique good?
- How do you get started?

What we're going to cover

My goal with this book is to give you an overview and a full run-through of the UX process alongside hands-on methods that you can apply straight away. Nothing is set in stone. You don't always have to follow a strict order, nor do you need to implement all of the methods in each step in order to be successful.

There are a ton of methods that are not included in this book; I only picked methods that can be easily implemented and easily applied to a wide range of projects. There are advanced techniques out there that are highly effective, but you'd need a seasoned professional or a crazy amount of effort to execute them successfully.

You should bear in mind that this book isn't intended to be the most "professional" UX book on the market. The goal is not to be scientific, and I'm not here to drown you in theory. Don't get me wrong; theory is important. But if you're starting with UX, you need to have some basic knowledge and an overview before you delve deeper into certain methods. The best way to learn about UX is to obtain an overview of the full process, understand some basic theory, then get lots of practice. After all that, you can work on refining your knowledge. I also recommend reading about cognitive and behavioral psychology, which will allow you to understand more about how users think and make certain choices.

Who is this book for?

One of my goals was to give product managers a great handbook. Even though they might not be the ones to execute the designs, they have to see through the process and coordinate the work. They have to work with designers, researchers, and developers and understand their roles and how to get the most out of the product team. *7STEPUX®* will give you a roadmap for a successful startup or enterprise product.

If you're a product manager, you'll find this book useful for introducing a complete process—from planning a product to designing and carrying out research to finally handing it over to the developers. You'll learn about the methods that you can use to coordinate the process and when to involve a team or an individual. Rest assured, I worked with several product managers on this book and incorporated their feedback to ensure that the content is useful for you.

This book also functions as a guide for designers. You might be a visual designer who wants to know more about UX or a UX designer who wants to expand your knowledge. If you're a designer, your first port of call should be the design related chapters. Great designers don't just focus on visuals but solve problems and care about user needs and business goals. This book will help you communicate better and, at the end of the day, it will help you become—and feel like—a much better designer.

I also wanted to create a helpful guide for business owners who know that UX plays a crucial role in a product's success. Any savvy businessperson will tell you that the execution is more important than the product. If you know this, and you want to focus on your product's success, you'll love this book. As a business leader, you'll understand the basic processes, who's who in the field of UX and product development, what UX is good for, and how to make product development measurable. You might be a startup CEO or a top manager in a faceless corporation. Either way, I'll help you get the most out of your product development efforts. For business owners, I recommend reading the *Get Started With UX* chapter. The *7STEPUX®* Process chapter will introduce the whole process. *The Plan* chapter will help you to see what it takes to plan a UX project. There's also the *Start Now!* chapter, which will help you implement UX within your company.

And, of course, this book is intended for anyone who's interested in the world of UX or anyone who's interested in developing a product. In my opinion, UX isn't just a quickly developing field; it's also something that's fun and very rewarding if you invest the time. At the end of the day, we want to solve other people's problems and make them happy by creating better products. In this book, I'll show you how to get started.

My FREE Gift to You

Access to the 7STEPUX® Resource Center

When I wrote this book, I knew it wasn't enough to "just write a book." One of the difficulties of getting started with UX is finding the right templates and the right form of documentation. For me, it took years to develop the User-Centered Business Canvas, the User Persona template, and all the various documents I use and need during the Design phase. All of these docs are essential for my work, yet I had to create most of them from scratch. I'm here to save you from those headaches! That's why I created the *7STEPUX® Resource Center*. This is where you'll find all the templates, guides, checklists, cheat sheets, and documents that I use for my work every day.

The resources are broken down and categorized by each chapter (Plan, Discover, Explore, etc.), making it super easy for you to find the relevant templates wherever you are in the process.

But there's more! Apart from the templates, I've included tons of recommendations and resource links for you to learn more about UX and design. I've included a special behind the scenes guide that reveals all the tools I use on a daily basis. Are you curious about which design tools I use for various UX-related activities? Do you want to know how I manage client work and the exact tools I use to make sure nothing falls through the cracks? If so, this guide is for you!

The 7STEPUX® Resource Center. A library built for UX work.

To get your hands on all the good stuff inside the *7STEPUX® Resource Center*, just follow this link:

csabahazi.com/7STEPUX-resource-center

How to use this book

I suggest you consider this book as an everyday handbook. It's not a book that you'll read once and condemn to a lifetime on the shelf. Here's what I recommend:

Read the parts that catch your attention. The order in which you read the chapters is not set in stone. However, there is a logical and somewhat chronological order here. But if something looks interesting to you, go ahead and check it out!

Explore the *7STEPUX® Resource Center!* Check out the various templates, the additional guides, and, of course, the forum itself. When you read about a method in the book, always go to the *Resource Center* and have a look at the related templates.

Choose the methods that you can apply from the book, then visit the *Resource Center!* You'll soon discover what kind of techniques and methods you need for your work. You'll read about how to do the planning, design, research, and test activities. Once you know what you want to do, go to the *7STEPUX® Resource Center* and select the resources that you need for the task at hand.

Keep this book with you! I designed this book to be handy for whenever you might need it. So, whenever you're planning a meeting or discussing a design problem, just open the book and find a solution.

Get Started With UX

UX in real life

Before we dive in and see how UX can help you make better digital products, let's find out what user experience really is. Most people think that UX is just a digital thing. Some think that UX people build websites or apps and that UX is a magic ingredient that you add to an existing product to make it great.

The truth is, UX has always been around, and it's not only important in the digital world. In real life, we're surrounded by user experience, think midi-chlorians (sorry, there are going to be some Star Wars jokes along the way). For example, when it comes to everyday objects, ergonomics plays an important role, which is an element of UX. How easy is it to use? Can you navigate your way through the product? If you can understand how a product works right away, it's a good UX. And, if something is easy to use and makes your life easier, you're going to love that product.

Doors with good UX. You just know how to handle them.

Take a look at these two doors. Do you know how to open them? Piece of cake, right? This is because they're ergonomic, and you're told how to use them.

When you go shopping, enter a building, or search for an item at home, you're a user. If you don't find something, if you get lost, or if you get frustrated because something doesn't work as it should, it's a bad UX. If you're brilliant enough to make sense of the case below, please feel free to email me.

Not sure what the idea behind this was...

UX is about the experience a user has while using a product or service (note that in the case of a service, it's better to call it service design, not UX design). This brings us to a simple fact: There's no such thing as having or lacking UX. You can only choose whether to pay attention to UX or ignore it. It's clear in the example above that the architect chose to ignore it.

Kazinczy, a famous Hungarian poet, once said, "Do great in a great way." This is an important idea to understand. UX is not just for creating something and serving it up. UX is about designing a good product that is good for users and good for business.

What is UX design?

Simply put, user experience is the total effect of actions the user goes through, feels, and thinks throughout their usage of the product or service.

However, you don't need to have "UX" in your title to pay attention to user needs. A helpful customer service representative also adds to the UX experience within a business. In this case, it's better known as "customer experience." This is because this term covers everything with regard to how that user or customer interacts with the business. Nevertheless, the principles are the same as in UX.

Apart from the fact that UX has a process and several methods, it's essentially a way of thinking about product development. If you're a UX-minded product manager, you don't decide what it is your users Want. Instead, you try to find out what they Need and build a solution that works for them. Trust me, good UX will support your business goals.

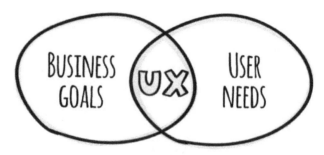

In the sweet spot between user needs and business goals, you'll find UX.

So UX is between two worlds; the Business Goals and the User Needs. From the user side of things, you want to uncover their needs, understand their problems, and solve those problems. In other words, you make their life easier by simplifying the tasks they have to carry out. You want to make them happy and engaged. On the business side, you strive to generate revenue, expand profit margins, grow market share, and acquire customers. In the sweet spot, you'll find UX.

Let's review some elements that make a good UX. If you do a quick search on Google for UX-related keywords, you'll end up seeing a lot of infographics and images. This is one of my favorites:

Simplest way to explain UX.

To better understand the elements of UX, we need to visualize it. If you read a little more about UX, you might come across an idea from Peter Morville that focuses on something called "UX Honeycomb." The honeycomb features the important elements of a meaningful and valuable user experience. However, I suggest a more visual approach. This is what I call my "UX Staircase."

You can see the users at the bottom of the stairs. Their goals are up at the top, so the users have to climb the stairs to reach their goals. But it's not just the goals that can be found up at the top. You'll also notice that the business goals are up there too. The stairs represent the user experience. Each step is an important element of UX.

The staircase of user experience.

Findable

Findability can mean a couple of things. It can be used to describe the way in which users find your product and how you make sure it reaches its intended target. This is mainly of importance to the marketing team. Nevertheless, you can apply findability within the product by asking the following question: Do users find the information they're looking for? Easy navigation will help people discover your product, making your product easier to find.

Accessible

When it comes to accessibility, most people think about blind or disabled users. Although there is much more to accessibility, in its purest form, it means that despite having a limited way of interacting with the product (usually some sort of disability), we can still access and use the product. Now, this can mean a wide range of things.

For example, there's a lack of accessibility if you're cooking in the kitchen and can only use one of your hands. Or, both of your hands are dirty because you're gutting a fish or making a sauce. Another limitation would be not having a high-tech cell phone or having an internet connection that's extremely slow. And, of course, we can't assume that all of our users have perfect eyesight. Just imagine your mom trying to read a letter with teeny-tiny text.

Usable

Usability ensures that the product is easy to use and appealing to the user. At the end of the day, every product is used by humans, each having their own feelings, emotions, needs, and frustrations. If a product is easy to use and engaging, people will spend more time with it. This can have a direct correlation with how the product is perceived and impact the pricing and positioning of the product. Imagine taking a trip in a standard car, then going out in a Bentley. Both cars will get you from A to B, but the experience you have during the trip is a completely different story.

Credible

To engage users, you have to build trust, and this comes down to credibility. For example, think about a payment page. If it doesn't seem trustworthy and legitimate, you probably won't want to enter your card details. Trust is one of the most important factors in UX. Do visitors believe what you say about your product? Does your brand (and product) appear trustworthy? Credibility and trust are important in the details as well. Do users believe and trust that you have the perfect product that will solve all their problems?

Useful

Lastly, is your product valuable to the users? Does it solve their problems in a way they would like them to be solved? This applies to the product as a whole. Every single feature must convey value to the user while meeting their needs. The core of UX is to identify user needs and address them. Therefore, design features and functionality are the only things that really matter to users when it comes to addressing their needs. Everything else is additional fluff, which has a bad effect on UX.

Back to our UX Staircase—imagine your users having to climb these stairs. It takes effort for them to scale all those stairs, so they have to be committed. Also, there's an order to the elements. If users don't find your product, they won't know if it's useful or not. If they can't access it, they'll abandon the whole thing. Bear in mind that the height of each step can vary. Not paying attention to usability or accessibility is like having a step that's too high. It's just a step, but it could mean the end of the journey for some users.

What makes a good UX?

Three things can make a good UX (in reality, it's more than that, but let's keep it simple). The first two things are to understand the user needs and the business goals. The third is to have a process that helps you in planning, researching, designing, and developing the product.

The success of UX lies in the process and the strategy you use. For this reason, I'm not going to tell you about all the different UX methods under the sun. Instead, I want to show you a whole process that you can follow. If your process is good, you will attain success.

They say that what sets amateurs and professionals apart is that the latter will reach the goal using a tried and true method. Meanwhile, the amateur will face uncertainty, and there will be gaps in the process. When it comes to product design, UX makes the process much more professional.

Understanding user needs is the foundation for a great product. However, sometimes it seems that the user needs and the business goals don't align well. Just think about ads on a website. If a business makes its money through advertising income, they can't not run ads just because ads annoy users (as they tend to do). In this case, you need the find the balance between the user experience and business goals.

Don't mess up on any of the steps; otherwise, you'll end up with a step that's too large for your users to take.

You could go above and beyond with making sure the ads are high quality and as relevant to the users as possible, or you could optimize the ads in a way that blends with the content better and avoids super annoying ad behaviors (like pop-up ads).

In the case of most products, it's not that difficult to align user needs with business goals. The reason we create products is to solve other people's problems. If you solve these problems in a way that suits the users, they're willing to pay for it. Everyone wins.

Roles in UX

In this book, I will refer to a variety of roles, such as visual designers, developers, and product managers. When it comes to UX, everyone seems to have different roles and titles, so I think it's best if we clear up the basics first. In order to help you better understand the roles, I will compare product design and development to constructing a house. This will help you understand who's who within the field of product development.

UX designer

The UX designer is the architect. They are in charge of understanding and interpreting the user needs and aligning them with the business goals. The UX designer should lead the design team and ensure that the process is focused on the user. In practice, the UX designer designs the information architecture, organizes information, and creates personas, task flows, and user journeys. They also collaborate with visual designers and UX researchers. A UX designer might draw wireframes as well, but they are normally focused on transforming user needs into product fundamentals. In short, the UX designer has to design the way in which the users will interact with the product.

A UX designer plays a key role on the team; they will have all kinds of project information concerning the design, findings from the research and test activities, and input from management.

UX researcher

Without a surveyor, you won't know if you're building your house on a solid foundation or in the middle of a swamp. In the same way, UX researchers are in charge of doing tests and research to better understand user needs and validate problems. A good researcher is a good psychologist. They will observe the users, collect feedback, and analyze and bring that valuable information to the table so that designers can use this knowledge to design a better product. (A UX designer can and should also do research activities. However, in a bigger team, it's worthwhile to create a separate role for research).

When it comes to testing the designs, it's best not to test your own. This is simply because you can easily become biased in this situation. As a designer, you're under time pressure, and you're always focused on the creation. You're deeply involved in the project. The goal of the tests is to find out whether you've created the right design and made the right product decisions or not. This has to be as objective as possible, so leave it up to the researcher.

Visual designer

The visual designer is the interior designer. They're often called UI (user interface) designers or even product designers. The visual designer comes in after the walls and other parts of the structure are built and starts designing the interior. A good interior designer will design your house according to your daily needs and habits. In the same way, a visual designer makes the product look great, engaging, and usable. The product's visual design will soon come to life thanks to the visual designer's creativity and magical flair.

The rise of the product designer

The field of UX and product design is constantly changing and evolving. After UX became popular, visual designers quickly jumped on the train and created the title "UX/UI designer." To be honest, I've never liked this term, since most UX/UI designers know nothing about UX, strategy, business, or research. This is just a fancy way for them to say, "I design stuff that people love." In the past few years though, another role has emerged—the product designer. A product designer has both the knowledge of a highly skilled UX professional and the abilities of a visual designer to create the final design for the product. The title also has "product" in it to indicate that the designer is responsible for creating the design from A to Z and not just drawing some bits and pieces. Usually, product designers specialize more in creating web and mobile applications and stay away from designing websites and marketing materials, and rightfully so, as understanding the business and working with a complex information architecture requires very different skills from drawing a logo.

I will make a lot of references to developers in my book, so let's clear this up as well. By "developers," I mean programmers who will take the finished designs, sit down, and transform them into fully functional code—in other words, a living digital product. There are two types of developers: front-end and back-end.

Front-end developer
In my house example, this is the person who finishes the drywall and lays the bricks. They build up the walls and the structure of the house. When it comes to digital products, we call these people the front-end developers. They break down the designs and code them so that browsers and/or mobile devices display the product. Everything that the user can see is described as "front-end."

Great front-end developers should also pay attention to UX since the output of their work is what users will see and interact with. There are details that are added here, such as transitions and animations, which also contribute to the overall UX of the product. But most importantly, this is the time when the interactions come to life, so the front-end developer has to make sure that everything is perfect.

Back-end developer
Back-end development is a bit like the plumber's fittings or the electrician's handiwork. The back-end programming can't be seen from the outside. This is what makes the product "work." For example, the design-

er creates a checkout form, the front-end developer creates that form so that it's in the web browser and you can fill it in, but behind that, there's nothing. If you hit "submit," nothing happens. This is when the back-end developer comes along and builds the database behind the product and connects it with the front-end (so when you hit "submit," the product sends the data to the database displaying a success message for the users and so on). To put it simply, back-end developers make the product "work."

Developers have a huge role to play when it comes to a product's success. At the end of the day, they're the ones who will build the product based on the input from the designers. Also, there are multiple factors that can affect UX that will only begin to surface after development (e.g., performance issues).

Have you ever found yourself waiting an eternity for a page to finally load? It might not look like a UX problem at first glance, but when you take a look at the analytics, you might see that you're losing a lot of visitors due to pages taking ages to load. Everything that affects the experience of the users is UX. If the page doesn't load, or if it takes a decade to load, that's a serious UX issue that needs to be addressed.

When it comes to UX, it should not be the sole responsibility of the UX designer. The more a team focuses on UX, the more a company can take better care of its users. For this reason, UX should be a team sport.

Why is UX essential for business?

A growing number of companies understand that UX is a key differentiator and that every dollar spent on UX will generate a return for the company. It's 100 times cheaper to fix a problem during the Design phase than it is to wait until it goes live and fix things after a product launch. According to surveys, by 2020, UX will be the key brand differentiator that will make or break a product's success. See how fortunate you are to be reading a book on UX right now? You're on track!

Not convinced yet? Let's dig a little deeper. Some people don't understand why there's a focus on UX. Therefore, I've listed a few reasons why UX is good and how it can affect business.

UX lowers the cost of product development.
Since we're involving the users in the process from the very early stages, we can eliminate a lot of mistakes, bad design decisions, and unnecessary features. By introducing UX, the first time you receive user feedback on the product will be early in the process.

In practice, this means that money spent on UX will generate savings on the development side. For example, it saves time and money if you don't have to develop unnecessary features. It's also a waste of time if developers have to correct mistakes that could have been avoided. As Conor Ward says, "The only thing more expensive than designing good experiences is designing bad experiences."

UX lowers the product risk.
Every design and new feature decision involves product risk. Is this design decision a good one? Will the users like this feature?

From a business perspective, we obviously want to lower this risk. UX research, data-informed thinking, and validating product decisions all serve one purpose—testing our product assumptions to help us make better decisions. This makes the process transparent and measurable. The risk comes in when you fail to validate your assumptions, which in turn creates a situation where the blind is leading the blind.

For example, a usability test with five participants can reveal around 85% of the usability issues. This can be done during the design process so you can eliminate these issues before going into development.

If something is easy to use, users will use it more often. This means more money for you and your business. If something is difficult to use, users will abandon it and move on to something else. Research shows that 68% of users abandon a product or company because they don't feel taken care of.

If the product is easy to use, users are more likely to return. This is why UX is not an obscure science but rather something real that has a direct impact on ROI (return on investment). According to a previous study, every dollar spent on UX generates 100 dollars in return.

Research by Forrester reveals that, for those companies focusing on UX, customers are 14% more likely to buy. UX lowers the chance of users changing brands by 15%, and it increases the likelihood of users recommending the product or service by 16%.

<u>Good UX makes your product easier to sell.</u>
If you've ever read anything about marketing, you've probably encountered this little saying: For good marketing, you need a great product.

This is true. It's easier to create a successful online campaign for a product that has a good conversion rate and is loved by users. A mobile app that's focused on user needs can generate more advertising revenue because the users continuously return to the app.

Good UX also plays a role in search engine marketing (SEO/SEM). For example, making the product easy to use will boost engagement with the product and bolster organic shares, thereby affecting the SEO.

<u>Good UX helps build better products.</u>
UX is all about creating better products. It's about creating better features, better development, and more satisfied users.

Your users will love the product, talk about it, and last but not least, you'll enjoy working on it.

So, if anyone asks you how they'll see a return on money invested in UX, tell them about some of the examples found here, or simply give them this book.

Plan · Discover · Explore · Define · Design · Validate · Deliver

The 7STEPUX® Process

UX is all about the process. You can use a lot of different methods and techniques. There are a wide range of UX research activities, and UX designers come up with new methods as they experiment with new techniques every day. Nevertheless, you should concentrate on the process and not on the individual methods. It's not the best wireframing tool, the most carefully crafted magical design, or the most exemplary prototype that makes UX successful and efficient. A good UX process will do this for you.

The *7STEPUX®* process ensures that we keep our focus and set goals, and it makes the process measurable in order to get the most out of the product. In the upcoming chapters, we'll cover the complete *7STEPUX®* process, and you'll see what kind of methods can be applied in each step.

If you know Design Thinking, this will be familiar to you. The concept behind this process is a very practical approach. It's always difficult to create a theory or methodology for UX that organizes things due to the wide range of ways to achieve good results.

I prefer to use the *7STEPUX®* process, which separates the different phases of the work (strategy, design, research, etc.) and indicates a clear focus for the given phase. Now, let's take a look at the process.

#1 Plan

First, we have to create the strategy behind the project. We need to set goals and the project scope and collect all the information that will be necessary during the project. Before we jump in and design the interface, we have to plot out and design the users' journey. We also need to determine the way the users will interact with the product. The goal of the Plan phase is to lay a solid foundation for the project.

#2 Discover

During the Plan phase, we might not know a lot about the users, and at this point, we might still have a lot of assumptions about the product. This is where we need to apply UX research and analytics to collect more data and validate our core assumptions—this is called the Discover phase. I should mention that the Plan and the Discover phases are usually complementary to one another. Sometimes you need to apply research right after starting the project because you don't have enough information. The order suggests that you have assumptions first, which will lead you to the type of research you'll need.

#3 Explore

Once you see the problems and needs, you can start to think about possible solutions. The Explore phase is really about experimenting with different approaches and sketching the first ideas. It's important that we not commit ourselves to a solution too early on. This is where we apply sketching and lo-fidelity prototyping to quickly materialize our ideas.

#4 Define

After we've designed the foundation and core structure for the product, we can move forward by breaking down the design and creating digital wireframes and prototypes. It's not just the technology that's different here. The main difference is that this is when we focus on the details. We refine the information architecture of the screen and focus on the copy, layout, and interactions. We'll use wireframes and digital prototypes to design and test these.

#5 Design

At this point, once the outline of the product is ready, we can add the visuals. This is when the product starts to shine with its images, typography, colors, and refined layout. But it's not just about aesthetics. We have to design the kind of feelings and emotions we want to communicate to the users. In addition, the visual design must support the structure and make it easier for users to understand how the product works. A good example of this is color coding. You can easily find out how a product works based on a black and white wireframe. But adding colors will also add an extra layer that helps you better understand the design. At this stage, we create visual designs and digital prototypes that will represent the final appearance of the product.

#6 Validate

We have to validate our design decisions before implementing them in development. In reality, this phase is more like a refining and iterating phase. For example, you run a usability test with the target audience, make changes to the product, and test again if necessary. For validating designs, we use first impression testing (e.g., five-second tests, usability tests, and A/B tests).

#7 Deliver

After testing, we hand the designs off to the developers who will break them down and create the coded product. After the product launch, we can measure and test how the product performs and incorporate the feedback from the users into a new product release. The Deliver phase is important in making sure the developers have everything they need to start their work.

A word about iteration

In this book, you'll frequently encounter the word "iteration." By iteration, I mean the process of designing something, validating it through testing, and creating a new "iteration." In other words, I mean creating a newly refined version by incorporating feedback and findings that emerged during the Validation phase.

This brings us to an important note with regard to the process. You'll see one Validate phase here; however, in reality, creating and testing out the designs is a constant process with many different stages and layers.

For example, when you create wireframes, it's best to conduct usability tests to uncover usability issues in the early stages of the design. At this phase, users can interact with the product (even though it's just in wireframes); this makes it a lot cheaper to eliminate issues and execute changes here, rather than later on.

So, let's say you've conducted a usability test on the wireframes. Now you have to further refine the wireframes based on the findings from the test; you should create a new iteration and test again, if necessary. Once you're satisfied with the wireframes, you can move forward and create the visual designs. Here, the same scenario comes into play—design, test, and create new iterations. We'll delve deeper into this particular topic when we reach the design related chapters.

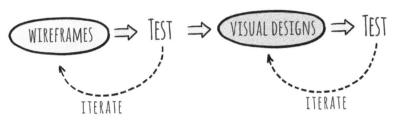

You have to validate both the wireframes and the visual designs.

Imagine building a house

Remember the different roles that exist in the world of UX? We can set up an analogy for the process as well. Building a house starts with careful planning. A great architect will consider two key things: (1) what the customer wants (user needs), and (2) what requirements the house should meet so that it doesn't collapse (business goals).

The architect will have a chat with us to uncover our wants, needs, and the possibilities that are available. When it comes to UX, it's important to observe the users and try to understand them. By doing this, we can create a great product for them.

The architect will start with the foundation and the outline of the house. They'll start creating the structure and frame and designing the core spaces, while resisting the temptation to start planning out the wallpaper and furniture (which isn't really part of their role anyway). In our case, we also start by designing the structure before we even begin to think about the visuals. A digital product's foundation is the information architecture, the layout, and the interactions.

When the walls are up, the interior designer will make an appearance. In real life, an interior designer is also a great UX designer. They have to know what their clients want and need, but they also have to be aware of the client's habits. Using this information, they can design a space for their clients in which they will feel at home. An interior designer sometimes ignores what the client says and, instead, creates something by observing the client and their behaviors. A great interior designer should not just draw up a list of what the client wants and then run off to buy everything. A great designer understands the client's needs and will design the kitchen, living room, etc. to meet those needs. When it comes to users, we don't really do everything according to their wish lists. Instead, we do research and observe the users. Then, based on that information, we can create the specific product that solves their problems.

Be flexible!

It's important to know that the seven steps don't necessarily follow each other in a strict order. I've already mentioned that we often begin to plan, then we immediately realize that we need to do UX research before moving forward. In the case of existing products, it's often best to start with testing and researching the current product to uncover problems. This way, you'll know how the product performs and where and what kind of issues emerge, which will allow you to think about how to address these issues.

In order to be very practical and hands-on during each step, we're going to cover the methods that you can use. Again, nothing is set in stone. The methods covered in this book are all practical and easy to start with; they're also applicable to a wide range of projects. However, within each phase, you have to select what specific methods you need for the current project. You don't always have to implement every method to be successful!

Every phase in the process represents a focus:

Step	Focus
Plan	Strategy
Discover	Collecting information
Explore	Idea generation
Define	Information architecture
Design	Visuality
Validate	Validating decisions
Deliver	Organizing and QA

It's better to use these phases than to try out a bunch of different methods one after another. The methods you use will vary from project to project. Nevertheless, the logical phases give you a solid foundation and a framework for the process.

Not just for building products from scratch

In its core form, the *7STEPUX®* process is about uncovering and understanding problems, generating possible solutions, and testing them out. Therefore, it can be used for many things, not just for creating new products from the ground up. You can use this process for improving existing products or even designing a single feature.

If you're designing a new product, the first two phases are crucial. In the *Plan phase*, you have to create the strategy for the product and plan the business part. During the *Discover phase*, you'll collect valuable information from the market and the users. The *Discover phase* will also help you validate your assumptions about the users and the business.

If you're improving an existing product, the *Plan phase* and the *Discover phase* will help you define the project's scope. This is where you have to review the existing product and analyze where you should start making improvements in order to enhance the product.

You can also apply this thinking to a single feature, because the process is exactly the same. You have to plan and ensure that there's a real need for the feature. Once you've done this, you'll need to collect feedback from the users, design the feature, and validate it.

All right, it's time to take a deep breath and dive into the *Plan* chapter. Are you ready? Here we go!

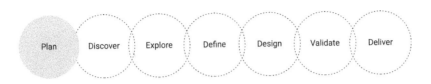

Plan · Discover · Explore · Define · Design · Validate · Deliver

#1 Plan
Create The Strategy Behind The Design

The Plan phase is about collecting information and creating the strategy for designing the product. This isn't easy—things can easily get out of hand if you spend too much time gathering data and interviewing stakeholders. On the other hand, if you don't set goals or define the scope of your project, you won't have relevant information ready; this could jeopardize the overall success of your project.

Also, let's be clear on what a "project" really is. When I say "project," I'm referring to a new product's first version, a redesign of an existing product, or simply designing a new feature. I use the term "project" to refer to something that's a process—begin, execute, and finish. Then, rinse and repeat.

Simply put, the Plan phase is about three things: (1) understanding user needs, (2) mapping out business goals, and (3) deciding what features and functionality should go into the product. Sounds easy as pie, right? It's also very important that everyone on the project understands the goals they want to achieve and that everyone feels comfortable with pitching their own ideas within the group.

Collecting data

One of the first things we need to do when planning a UX project is collect all the information that's relevant and that will be useful later on. Data is also important for understanding what kind of research we need based on the assumptions we have.

Planning helps lay out the ideas and goals for the project.

Stakeholder interview

One important resource is a stakeholder interview. Stakeholders have a wealth of knowledge regarding the product, market, goals, and requirements. At this point, we're not making design decisions or creating plans. Instead, we're focused on collecting ideas, requirements, and business goals that are directly related to the project.

You can interview the relevant product stakeholders on a one-to-one basis. However, from my personal experience, I find it's best to run a workshop in which all stakeholders share their opinions and ideas. By doing this, we can clarify what we're aiming to achieve. Limit the workshop to four or five stakeholders to allow for a more controlled environment, ensuring a more focused result.

Analytics and data

Collecting big data now and having a data team can be extremely useful when you get to the Design phase. You can answer a lot of questions about the users and their behaviors as well as good and bad things about the current product by examining the data you have. This is not only true for big data. If you have any sort of analytics (e.g., Google Analytics), it's a good idea to analyze it first. The data can be used to validate assumptions about the user personas (such as demographics and behaviors), and it can also help you identify problems with the product.

Desk research

I'm sure you've heard of desk research. This is when we use the internet (or any other existing resource for information) to look up relevant data for the project. This doesn't take a lot of time, and it can be quite useful.

Desk research also involves taking a look at the competition to see their strengths and weaknesses. Here are a few things that you might want to do desk research for:

- Analyzing your competitors
- Looking for existing solutions for a problem

- Seeing what users are searching for (this might help validate a problem)
- Learning about what there is to know about the users

You can use Google (Search, Trends), Facebook (or other social media platforms where your target audience hangs out), Quora, or any other resources to dig deep and find answers.

Customer support tickets and user feedback

Most people don't realize that extremely valuable information can be extracted by analyzing the customer support tickets. But if you think about it, those tickets are actual, real-life pieces of feedback on your product. They tell you what's good and what's bad about it. It's worth reviewing the tickets, the feedback from the users, the reviews, and the ratings of the product. In addition, if you offer customer support, it's a good idea to invite a representative for a brainstorming session. They have valuable information about the users (e.g., who they are, what they want, and what they like and dislike about the product). This information will help you better understand the product and define the project scope.

UX research to apply:

<u>User interviews</u>
Conduct user interviews; they're great for understanding what your users need, think, and feel. They provide valuable information that you can use to create better user personas.

<u>A usability test</u>
If you have an existing product but don't know where to start, do-

42

ing an initial round of usability testing can go a long way. You'll see the users interacting with the product and be able to observe and discover usability issues. Based on this, you'll end up with a prioritized list of things you need to change in the product.

The User-Centered Business Canvas

It's challenging to see all aspects of the business. You have marketing standpoints, product ideas, business requirements, and user needs. Although we're designing a product, and UX is about the users, we mustn't forget that this is a business, after all. Let me repeat that: UX is about aligning user needs with business goals. A great tool for visualizing every aspect of the product is the User-Centered Business Canvas. If you've read anything about the lean method (e.g., The Lean Startup by Eric Reis), you're already familiar with the Lean Canvas template.

The idea behind the User-Centered Business Canvas is that it puts the user in the center. It combines the essential ingredients of a product: the problem, the user, and the product.

Why do you need a User-Centered Business Canvas (UCBC)?

- The UCBC is a great way to start a project and begin planning a product. It will give you an overview of the whole product and the foundations of the experience.
- Everyone on the team (and in the company) will see how the product works—on both the business side and the user side.

- It draws your attention to crucial things you have to think about (e.g., the fears of your potential clients and who the early adopters of the product or feature would be).

THE PROBLEM		THE USER		THE PRODUCT	
PROBLEMS, NEEDS	**USERS**	**USER FEARS**	**SOLUTION**		**ACQUISITION CHANNELS**
- Hard to find a meeting time the suits everybody - Have to use website to look up this information - not handy enough - Need to access it quickly, during a meeting - Needs to remember the settings so won't have to start over and over again - hard to find a dates in a non-visual interfaces - Have to consider holidays, winter and summertime as well	- People who often organize meetings and calls with people in different timezones - Teams doing the same - Telcom companies and remote working companies	- Will mess up something and get the wrong time - The product won't know holidays, special days and summer time/winter time differences - Can't find the right time for everybody	- a mobile and desktop app which comes handy whenever you need it - have presets to save time and the app learns your schedule - show proof that the products take care of everyhing (summeritme etc.) - visual interface to find the matching times easier		- target the users of the existing sites (display ads) - content marketing using relevant content (blogs) - target time-saving and remote working related content sites
					REVENUE SOURCES
					- app purchases - premium functionality (automatic learning) - ad revenue from relevant, targeted ads (eg productivity tools) - affiliate marketing in content
EXISTING SOLUTIONS	**EARLY ADOPTERS**	**USER GOALS**	**VALUE PROPOSITION**		
- converter sites - hard to access, not handy enough, can't store data and remember frequent settings	- Remote working agencies, IT companies with global clinetele - managers, product owners who communicate regularly (many times a week) - people who use the existing websites frequently or tried a mobile solution	- Find a time that suits everybody in the most quickest and convenient way possible - Spent the least time with it - look professional and organized	Hourly solves the problem of organizing across the globe meetings for teams in different timezones in an easy to use and intiuitve way.		**METRICS**
					- number of returning users in a given time period - number of app downloads in a given time period

The User-Centered Business Canvas.

How do I use a UCBC?

Use the UCBC for every project, and remember to keep it up to date! I love to fill in this canvas as a kick-off for a project. At the beginning, there are lots of assumptions and questions regarding the product (especially if it's a brand-new product). By filling in the canvas, you can map out these questions and assumptions; this will force you to prioritize and validate them based on how much business risk those assumptions involve.

Later in the process, we'll create user personas to represent the target users. It's much easier to do this by starting with a canvas. Start with the big picture, then think about the users in relation to the problems and existing solutions; it's just easier to brainstorm this way.

Keep it up to date!

The canvas is not something that you do once and then forget about. In the beginning, you'll use a lot of assumptions when filling in the canvas. You have to validate those assumptions and refine the canvas. For example, if you do user interviews (covered in the next chapter), they'll be a source for validating information about the users and adding new ones as well.

How to fill in the canvas?

The canvas has three main sections: the problem, the user, and the product. The user is the one in the middle, that's why we call it "user centered." Smart, no? Although there's a logical order for the sections, sometimes you have to jump back and forth during the brainstorming—and that's fine. A good way to begin is to start with the problems or the user section, whichever appeals to you or is the one you have the most information or ideas about. For example, if you start with the user, you can ask yourself, "What kind of problems do they experience?" If you start with the problems, you can ask yourself, "Who might experience these problems?"

Okay, let's fill in that canvas. As an example, we're going to fill in the canvas for an online tool that helps people in different time zones find a meeting time that's good for everyone. You can access the full, filled-in canvas in the *7STEPUX® Resource Center*, which will help you get the hang of how it works.

Problems/Needs section

What problems do users face? What needs do they have? List the top, most painful problems and urgent needs of the users. You can use the findings from stakeholder interviews and customer service inputs and brainstorm your own ideas. User interviews and observations can bring in more insight and validate this information.

EXAMPLE:

- Hard to find a meeting time the suits everybody in different time zones
- Need to access it quickly (e.g., during a meeting)
- Have to consider holidays and seasons

Existing Solutions section

Here, we input what kind of solutions users have aside from our product. This involves the competitors' products. However, sometimes there's no real alternative. For example, if you were to automize something that people can do only with pen and paper, the existing solution is pen and paper. Don't simply list the competing products! Instead, focus on the weaknesses. What's missing? In what ways do the competing product not fulfill the customers' needs?

EXAMPLE:

- Use of competitor website: hard to access, lots of clicks
- Doesn't remember settings: have to do it over and over again
- Hard to find matching times in a nonvisual interface

Users section

Who are the mainstream users? What's there to know about them? If you have multiple user types, you can feature them here. However, from a business perspective, it's best to focus on the paying user (most likely one persona). Don't go into too much detail here. We'll do that when we create the user personas. Try to list only the most important, most distinctive attributes of the users.

EXAMPLE:

- People and teams who often organize meetings and calls with people in different time zones
- Telecommunication companies who embrace working remotely
- Geographically distributed teams

Early Adopters section

Early adopters are the first and best customers. They'll pay for the earliest viable version of your product. This is because they suffer from the problems the most. Early adopters are aware of their problems, and most likely, they're on the hunt for solutions. Maybe they're using a competing product (or have abandoned one), or maybe they're building their own solution. These people are extremely important since you're going to build the business around them (at first). They'll come and test the product, give you feedback, and pay for the first version.

EXAMPLE:

- Remote working agencies; IT companies with global clientele
- Managers; product owners who communicate regularly (many

times a week)
- People who use the existing websites frequently or tried a mobile solution but stopped using it (because it wasn't handy)

User Fears section

Users not only have positive feelings but also fears and worries. These are also important for the product. For example, speaking of an SAAS (software as a service) product, users might fear that it will be too complex and time consuming for them to learn, or maybe they worry that they won't be able to migrate their data if they switch to new software. These fears have to be addressed from the product side and in the marketing. So ask yourself, *What do my customers fear? What are they worried about?* This can be related to the product and also to the problems they experience.

EXAMPLES:

- Might mess something up and get the wrong time
- Product won't adjust for holidays, special days, and summer/winter time changes
- Won't be able to find the right time for everybody

User Goals section

What motivates the users? What are their goals? What do they want to achieve? It's a good idea to keep user needs and goals separate. User goals are not really about what they "want," in essence, but rather what outcome they hope to get. You have to uncover their needs and understand their goals so that you can design a product that fulfills their needs and helps them reach their goals.

- Find a time that suits everybody in the quickest and most convenient way possible
- Spend the least amount of time with organizing
- Be perceived as professional and organized

Solution section

Here, you will list the top solutions that will solve user problems. List feature ideas and functionality. How can you solve the user problems? How could the product help them reach their goals? The challenge is that you don't have much space. You have to address these problems and goals with four to five bullet points.

EXAMPLE:

- A mobile and desktop app that comes in handy whenever you need it
- Presets to save time and an app design that learns the user's schedule
- Show proof that the product takes care of everything (e.g., adjusting for time changes.)
- A visual interface to make time matching easier

Value Proposition section

What's the biggest value users get from the product? What sets you apart from your competition? The best way to approach this is to write your answers in a sentence or two.

Hourly solves the problem of organizing meetings across the globe for teams in different time zones in an easy to use and intuitive way.

Acquisition Channels section

How do you acquire new customers? What kind of channels can you use to reach your audience? Here you can list your ideas for marketing. The canvas will force you to think in context and not be too vague, such as saying, "We'll use social media." You've defined your users and your early adopters. Which social media platform do they hang out on? Can you use ads to reach them, or is it more like a direct sales approach? Also, you may need different marketing channels in the early stages of the product as opposed to later in the life cycle.

EXAMPLE:

- Target the users of the existing sites (e.g., using AdWords display ads)
- Content marketing using relevant content
- Target time-saving and remote working related content sites and resource list blog posts

Revenue Sources section

How do you make money? How is the product monetized? Since this is an SAAS tool, it might be as simple as subscription fees. But in most cases, you have multiple options for monetization. In addition, you might use different monetization at the start than you'll use in later phases. For example, you can launch a product with only the monthly/yearly subscription fees, and later you can add premium functionality that users can buy as an extra. Your team will be better able to focus on outcomes when they understand how the project is going to make money.

EXAMPLES:

- App purchases
- Premium functionality (e.g., machine learning features)
- Ad revenue from relevant, targeted ads (e.g., productivity tools)
- Affiliate marketing

Metrics section

Metrics are about measuring the success of the product. The question is, which metric will tell us if the product is successful? We'll go into this in more detail in a moment, and I'll show you an easy way to come up with useful metrics for the product. You'll need different metrics at different stages of the product. For example, the number of new customers in a given period is a good place to start. The number of beta sign-ups would also be helpful. But when you move forward, you'll need to focus on activating these users and retaining them; you'll need another metric, such as retention rate.

EXAMPLE:

- Number of returning users in a given time period
- Number of app downloads in a given time period

Have a workshop!

Duration	Who to invite	Prepare
2–3 hours	Product manager Designer Stakeholders Marketers Researchers Customer service reps	Whiteboard Sharpies Post-its UCBC template

1. Prepare.

Book a meeting room for two to three hours and invite the participants. You can invite product managers, designers, marketers, and stakeholders. Keep it limited to five to six participants so the workshop doesn't take up the whole day.

Collect every bit of data that might come in handy during the workshop (e.g., desk research, customer feedback, and analytics). Draw the canvas on the whiteboard.

2. Introduce the User-Centered Business Canvas to the team.

Explain to the team why they're there and why their knowledge is important. Go through the canvas and explain each section so it's clear to everyone. If you have collected data, share it with the team and talk about it.

3. Brainstorm.

Go through each cell step by step and brainstorm ideas. Start with the problem or with the user cell. If it's a smaller team (one to three people), you can discuss each cell together. If you have a larger team, use a brainstorming technique (see below).

Give Post-it notes and Sharpie pens to the participants, then work independently for five minutes, brainstorming as many ideas on the Post-it notes as you can. It's important not to criticize the ideas during the first round because this round is about idea generation. Later, you'll have time to sort them out. Sometimes, the best solutions come from ideas that seem crazy at first mention.

4. Present and discvuss ideas.

When the five minutes are up, put the Post-its on the whiteboard one at a time. The participant who wrote the given Post-it should explain to the others what the idea is about and why they think it's relevant. Then, go to the next cell and start over. The goal is to brainstorm ideas for all of the cells.

5. Finalize.

Finally, when you're done, you'll have to digitize the canvas. In the *7STEPUX® Resource Center*, you'll find a template for this. Take a photo of the whiteboard and fill in the template. One important note here: Fill in the canvas in a way that's clear and understandable for everyone on the team (even for those who were not present at the workshop). You may have used a lot of abbreviations and keywords while writing on the Post-its, but when you create the digitized "final" version, refine the ideas, merge duplicates, and be very clear with the wording.

User Personas

A user persona is a fictive character that represents the targeted users. Usually, there are multiple personas for a product. They can differ in how they use the product, what problems they experience, or basically who they are. For example, if you think about a freelancing site, like Fiverr, there are at least two personas: the freelancers and the clients who look for talented freelancers. We use these personas to empathize with and understand the users.

Some people think personas—and persona profiles—are useless (what's the point of filling out a paper with mere assumptions?). Well, it's true that there will mostly be assumptions at first, but the game isn't over. We have to validate those assumptions and refine the persona based on UX research. A persona profile (using the User Persona template) should be a living, constantly updated document.

The persona...

- showcases the most important and relevant information about the users,
- helps us recruit participants for the UX research,
- shows the user needs and goals. We will use these to design a great product for them,
- describes real people (or a group of people)—their background, knowledge, and motivation, and
- reminds you that behind every product, there are human beings with feelings, desires, goals, and limitations.

Why should I use a User Persona template?

As a **product manager**, it will help you focus on the user, come up with better feature ideas, and prioritize them. By maintaining and updating the persona, you can eliminate irrelevant features and focus every meeting and discussion on the product and its users.

As a **UX designer**, you'll use the information that the persona showcases to design processes and decide what research activities you need and what you have to consider during the Design phase (e.g., where, when, and how the product would be used).

As a **UX researcher**, you'll recruit participants for tests and research based on the personas, then you'll use the findings of the research to refine the personas.

As a **visual designer**, the personas will give you an understanding of "who" the target audience is and what previous knowledge and expectations they have so you can tailor the visuals to their needs.

As a **marketing specialist or copywriter**, you can form the messaging based on what you know about the users. Fears and problems are extremely useful in marketing communication. It's even better when you have solid, validated knowledge about these fears and problems (and not just assumptions).

There are hundreds of different personas. There are marketing personas, sales personas, and various product personas. Here, we're going to use a persona that showcases only the must-have details about the users. We can use this for the research and design. However, as mentioned above, these personas are great for other uses as well. Bear in mind that it's important to keep the personas flexible.

If you think you need to add extra information, go ahead and do so. Most of the products can be covered by two to three personas. The really complex products can take up to four personas. Just try to keep the number of personas as low as you can. By adding new ones, you lose focus. Let's look at how to build up a user persona.

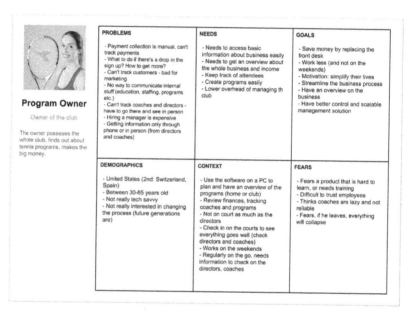

	PROBLEMS	NEEDS	GOALS
Program Owner Owner of the club The owner posseses the whole club, finds out about tennis programs, makes the big money.	- Payment collection is manual, can't track payments - What to do if there's a drop in the sign up? How to get more? - Can't track customers - bad for marketing - No way to communicate internal stuff (education, staffing, programs etc.) - Can't track coaches and directors - have to go there and see in person - Hiring a manager is expensive - Getting information only through phone or in person (from directors and coaches)	- Needs to access basic information about business easily - Needs to get an overview about the whole business and income - Keep track of attendees - Create programs easily - Lower overhead of managing th club	- Save money by replacing the front desk - Work less (and not on the weekends) - Motivation: simplify their lives - Streamline the business process - Have an overview on the business - Have better control and scalable management solution
	DEMOGRAPHICS	CONTEXT	FEARS
	- United States (2nd: Switzerland, Spain) - Between 30-65 years old - Not really tech savvy - Not really interested in changing the process (future generations are)	- Use the software on a PC to plan and have an overview of the programs (home or club) - Review finances, tracking coaches and programs - Not on court as much as the directors - Check in on the courts to see everything goes well (check directors and coaches) - Works on the weekends - Regularly on the go, needs information to check on the directors, coaches	- Fears a product that is hard to learn, or needs training - Difficult to trust employees - Thinks coaches are lazy and not reliable - Fears, if he leaves, everything will collapse

The User Persona template: Here you can find all the information you need to design a great product.

Picture, name, title, description

After you've created your personas, give them all names. This makes it easier to refer to them later on (e.g., "Joe would love this new feature!"). Finding a relevant photo also adds to the personality. The title can be a role (e.g., "event manager") or job title. But get creative on this one. You can create a title that best describes the user. When I was working with a big online magazine, we named the personas after the traffic source they visited the site from (e.g., "Facebook guy"). This was handy because the behavior and attitude of the users differed depending on how they got to the site.

You might also add a quick description explaining the role of the persona. For example, if you differentiate the personas based on what they do inside the product, it's good to dedicate a few sentences to explain these roles.

Problems

Problems (or pain points) are one of the most important aspects of a persona. List the main problems encountered in this type of user experience. These are the problems that you want to solve with the product. Furthermore, from these problems, you can derive the persona needs and goals (or the other way around).

Questions to ask yourself:

- What kind of problems do these people face?
- What makes their lives difficult?

Needs

Problems and needs are often connected. For example, if my problem is that it's impossible to keep track of administrative things in my business, I have a need for organizing, simplifying, and maybe automating these things. Note that these are not what people "want," but it's what they need in order to solve their problem.

You can be general (e.g., "needs a way to lower the amount of time spent on administration" or more specific (e.g., "needs a way to migrate existing data easily").

Goals

Mapping out the goals of the users is also crucial. The goals cover what end result or outcome the users are looking for. It's important to distinguish needs, goals, and what users say they want. You have to understand and focus on what outcome they would like to achieve. Sticking to the administration example, the users might say, "I want a tool that mostly automates the administrative tasks." Now, this is not a goal. The goals here would be that they want to save time, do less administration, or avoid mistakes and rework.

Questions to ask yourself:

- What goals do the users have?
- What outcome are they looking for?

Demographics

In the demographics section, we enter information about gender, age, location, and job responsibilities. Enter everything that describes who the user is—we're going to recruit people based on these criteria. If you have existing analytics or data, you should use that data to fill in this section. As a rule of thumb, only enter data that is relevant and can be used during design and research. For example, don't include their favorite TV show unless it's somehow related to the project.

<u>Questions to ask yourself:</u>

- What is the age of the target audience?
- What is their gender (mostly)?
- What is their professional background? Job responsibilities?
- What do they do on a daily basis?
- How do they collect information about similar products or related to their problems? Who do they ask for help?
- What are the typical traits of these people? Are they risk takers or risk avoiders? Are they tech savvy or tech dummy? Are they organized or spontaneous? Etc.

Context

The context can refer to the context of usage (where, when, and how they would use the product) and the context of how they experience the problems we aim to solve (where, when, and how they experience them). The context of usage covers the 360-degree scope of circumstances in which they use the product. For example, if you're going to design a cooking application, it's likely that the product will be used in the kitchen. Therefore, the users probably want to use it on a mobile device, but they can only use one hand, or they might not even want to touch the screen because their hands might be dirty. Knowing this, you can address these issues with the design (e.g., touch-friendly screens and perhaps voice control).

You can discover the context of usage with user interviews and observations. These research techniques will give you more insight and validate your existing assumptions about the context.

- How are they currently solving the problem?
- Why are they viewing my product?
- When and how will they discover the product (e.g., from Facebook, search engines, or browsing the app store lists)?
- What device will they use to access the product (e.g., cell phone, laptop)?
- What kind of software and tools are they familiar with (you can build upon this knowledge)?
- What prior knowledge do they have about my product or the existing solutions and competing products?

Fears

Lastly, we have to list the fears of the users—just as we did with the User-Centered Business Canvas. Remember, fears can be connected to the problems the users experience or toward a product or solution. It's important to think of both. Later in the process, when you think about functionality and marketing communication, fears will be important. You have to double check that you've addressed these fears with functionality, content, and communication.

Questions to ask yourself:

- What fears do users have?
- What are they worried about?

Expert advice: Map out functionality relevant to each user persona

When you're organizing information and collecting functionality, it's helpful to put the user in the middle and collect the relevant features and functions that the given user type would use or benefit from; this way, you're connecting each functionality to real user needs and goals.

Questions to ask yourself:

- Which features and functionality does the given user need?
- How could we solve the specific user needs?
- What is the biggest benefit in the product for the specific user?

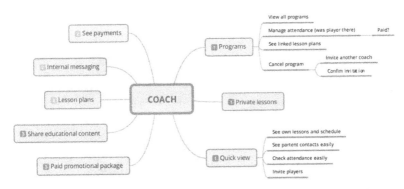

Draw a mind map for each user persona and group the features that are relevant to them.

Proto-personas

As you can see, we need a bit of information to enter into the User Persona template. But, if you think about it, we missed a beat—what if you don't know how many different personas you should create? If this is the case, create proto-personas. The point of proto-personas is to come up with different user types and sort them out so you can start creating the detailed user personas we discussed earlier. So, in essence, creating proto-personas is a brainstorming exercise.

Step one: Brainstorm!

The first step is to brainstorm as many different user types as possible. It's as simple as that. Grab a sheet of paper, divide it into four equal parts, and jot down four mini-personas. Since this is about idea generation, it's best to have a workshop. Invite the product managers, stakeholders, designers, and marketers.

PERSONA NAME	PERSONA NAME
Give a title	Give a title
My problem is...	My problem is...
I want to...	I want to...
PERSONA NAME	**PERSONA NAME**
Give a title	Give a title
My problem is...	My problem is...
I want to...	I want to...

Creating proto-personas will help you identify different user groups.

For each of the mini-personas, enter four key bits of information:

Name:
You have to call the kid something, and the name can provide a lot of information. A name can tell you about the persona's gender or even refer to an attribute (e.g., "Impatient John").

Title:
The title can be a job title, position, or location, but be creative on this one. You can use titles to enrich the persona and add bits of information. For example, you can use persona titles, such as "Facebook user," "Frequent coffee buyer," or "Tennis court owner."

My problem is...
Most of the users can be split up by the types of problems they experience. I mean, demographics are important, because teenagers and forty-somethings use the same devices completely differently. But most of the time, the problem and goals are the differentiators. You need to know and understand the problems first in order to come up with a solution. So quickly jot down a sentence explaining the specific problem or frustration these type of users experience.

I want to...
The other cornerstones of design are needs and goals. You can complete the "I want to..." sentence to reflect the most important user needs or describe the user's goals. Uncovering different user goals will help you prioritize and identify certain user types.

Step two: Prioritize!

Once you have your proto-personas, you have to prioritize and select the ones that you want to further refine and create user personas from them. Remember, you have to limit the number of personas to two or three (having more than that will lead to a loss in focus). Just take a look at the User Persona template. How much time do you think it would take for you to fill out 10 personas? Yep, pretty much that. So be tough; prioritize ruthlessly.

- Dump the irrelevant or duplicated personas.
- Merge the ones with overlaps. At this stage, demographics isn't really important since we know little to nothing about the users. So, for example, if you have two personas with the same problem—but the gender or age is different—skip that. It's one persona at this stage.
- Choose the most relevant ones for the project! Who is the paying user? Which user type would be an early adopter for the product?

The goal of proto-personas is to get you started with a few specific user types that you can move forward with and use to create a detailed user persona from.

Validating the user personas

The methods discussed above are great ways to identify your users and gather your initial assumptions about them. But you have to keep them as assumptions until you have proof that they're valid. Why? Because if you have an invalid assumption about the users' problems, this could easily mean that you've solved the wrong problem for them.

Risk comes in when you don't have information on something that could affect the product and the business. The less you know about the personas, the higher the potential risk is. This can have a big impact on the product (possibly in a very negative way). So go through your personas—start with the paying user—and identify the assumptions that would get you into trouble if you were wrong about them.

For example, if you're going to build a mobile app because you think the solution for the problem would be a mobile product, then there's a potential risk unless you have proof of two things: (1) The problem really exists and hurts the users bad enough to look for a solution, and (2) they want to use it on a mobile device for some reason. You have to know these to be true—and, the earlier the better.

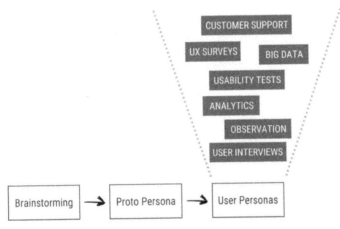

When you create your personas, apply UX research and data to validate your assumptions.

To validate the information in your personas, you have to apply analytics and UX research. We'll discuss these methods in length in the next chapter, but let's do a quick overview of which techniques you can use to validate personas.

User interviews

Interviews are the most common and best way to collect information about the users and validate your assumptions. This is the moment of truth. Meet and talk with your users, uncover their problems, and understand their needs and their goals.

Observation

Observation means that you go out to where your customers are and see how they're currently solving the problem. This is a great way to get to know more about the users and observe their behaviors.

Analytics, big data

Analytics and big data can be used to validate and add information to the Demographics section and the Context section of the persona. By analyzing user behavior, you can also come up with problems regarding the product or see a need in cases when the users don't find something they're looking for.

Usability tests

When testing the product with real users, you also have an opportunity to gather input for the personas. During a usability test, users are interacting with the product, doing tasks, and expressing their opinions. You can get feedback on the users' prior knowledge and the context of usage. Fears and needs can even surface during a usability test.

Customer service

Talking to customer service representatives in your company and analyzing the tickets, emails, or other materials they have can also validate assumptions about the users. Most of these inputs will be problems, such as what the users are unhappy about with the current product and maybe what features they're missing.

<u>UX Surveys</u>

Creating surveys and sending them out to potential users can also get you closer to them. This is especially useful if you don't have the opportunity to do interviews. Come up with a bunch of open-ended questions, send them out to potential users, and see if the results validate or invalidate your assumptions of the persona.

Do a workshop!

Duration	Who to invite	Prepare
1–2 hours	Product manager Designer Stakeholders Marketers Researchers Customer service reps	Whiteboard Sharpies Post-its User Persona template

1. Prepare.

Book a meeting room with a whiteboard for a few hours and invite participants. An ideal size for the workshop is four to five people. Don't invite more people; otherwise, the workshop will become clunky. Bring all the data and insight that could add value to the personas: analytics, big data reports, and/or any other data you have on your users.

Draw the six sections of the persona (Problems, Needs, Goals, Demographics, Context, and Fears) on the whiteboard. If you have multiple personas, draw this as a table with the columns being the different user types and the rows representing each section of the persona.

2. Brainstorm.

Explain to the attendees what the workshop is about and what you're going to do. Go through and explain each section of the persona and give hints on how to fill them in. You can print out the questions we discussed earlier, and that can serve as a cheat sheet.

Work independently for 10 to 15 minutes. Ask the participants to brainstorm ideas for each section of the persona and write each idea on a Post-it. The goal is to have as many ideas as possible. Don't start selecting ideas; don't throw away the bad ones. Just brainstorm.

You can do the brainstorming one of two ways. You can either pick a category to focus on, or you can let everybody freely brainstorm in any category they like. If you choose to go through the categories one by one, it's best to start with the Problem section, then continue with the Needs and Goals.

3. Discuss and iterate.

When time's up, ask participants to place each Post-it on the whiteboard in the category it belongs to and explain the idea. Rinse and repeat until you have enough information in every category and every persona (if there are multiple personas).

4. Finalize the personas.

By the end of the workshop, you'll end up with a few dozen Post-its. The next step is to sort the information out and create the digital persona. For this, use the User Persona template from the *7STEPUX® Resource Center*. Take a photo of the whiteboard or collect the Post-it notes so you can sit down and start to digitize them.

When creating the digital user persona, sort out the redundant ideas and merge the duplicates. Also, pay close attention to the wording. During the workshop, it's common for people to use abbreviations since there's very limited space on a Post-it. But when you fill in the digital persona, make sure the ideas are understandable and make sense to everybody (even those who were not present at the workshop). When you're ready, print out the personas, put them on the wall, and ask for feedback from your team and inside the company. Keep it as a living document, validate the assumptions in it, and keep it up to date.

Expert advice: Using Post-its.

I know this will sound like a no-brainer, but there are a few tips and tricks about using Post-its. When you write on a Post-it, use capital letters and make sure it's legible. Think ahead. You'll take a photo and digitize it later, so please avoid using Sanskrit. Sharpies work better than regular pens or pencils, which are hard to read. Use the space available, and make the text as large as possible. Lastly, don't free the Post-it from the stack from the bottom up (because it will bend and fall off of whatever surface it's on). Instead, turn the stack and pull the Post-it from the side. This way it will remain straight, won't bend, and can be attached to any surface. You didn't think there was that much to Post-it notes, did you?

PULL FROM THE SIDE

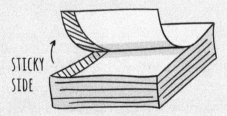

STICKY
SIDE

Pull the Post-it notes from the side instead of from the bottom up. This way, they won't fall off or bend. I know... It's pure magic.

Mapping out the functionality

Once you have the strategy and goals set, it's time to decide what goes into the product. The emphasis is on "what" and not on "how." Basically, a user can do two things inside the product:

- Use a function (do something)
- Consume content (see, listen, or read something)

A function is something the user can use and interact with. In our time zone converter app, the functionality allows the user to select different time zones, find matching times, save presets, and so on. We have to gather every functionality that we need to design. Aside from functionality, there's content. When I say content, I'm referring to any sort of content the user can consume (e.g., text, images, or videos). Put simply, content is information that we show to the users for a specific reason.

When we brainstorm functionality and content, we come up with ideas that solve the users' problems and fulfills business goals. If you're dealing with a web or mobile app, you'll most likely brainstorm features and functionality that enable the users to accomplish certain tasks. If you're designing a website or landing page, you'll mainly focus on the content the users have to see to move forward in the process (e.g., sign up and/or buy something).

At this stage, I'm sure you already have a lot of ideas on what features you should have in the product. Sometimes the most challenging part of the Plan phase is to not jump in and start to flesh out the ideas you have. The best way to come up with great ideas is to make the user the starting point for brainstorming. Take a look at each persona and ask yourself:

- What feature would solve the persona's problem?
- What feature is the persona looking for?
- What type of content do they need?
- What content would help resolve fears regarding the product?
- What information are they looking for?

Grab some Post-its!

The easiest way for brainstorming is to just use a whiteboard and Post-its. Put your user personas on the whiteboard, and start to write functions and content ideas on each of the Post-its. A little hack is to use different colored Post-its for function and content ideas. This way, you can play around with ideas and see if all the business goals and user needs are covered.

DASHBOARD			CONTACTS		
EMPTY STATE	OWNER	DIRECTOR	CONTACT LIST	CONTACT DETAILS	CREATE GROUP
WHAT'S NEXT?	YEARLY REVENUE	PROGRAM NAME	FIRST + LAST NAME	NAME	GROUP NAME
FB REQUEST	MONTHLY REVENUE	LOCATION	PHOTO	SEND EMAIL	ADD CONTACTS
	WEEKLY REVENUE	ATTEN-DANCE	MEMBER?	PHONE NUMBER	

Use a whiteboard or the wall to collect your Post-its. This way, you'll have a nice overview.

Prioritize ruthlessly!

UX is mostly about prioritization. When it comes to features, we have to prioritize ruthlessly. Go through each of the functions and ask yourself, Do I absolutely have to have this? If it's a new product, I like to ask my clients, "Okay, if you don't have this feature, can you still go to market?" You'd be surprised how much functionality and content can be cut back while still giving you a great first version of the product.

Identify potential business risks.

After you know what functionality you want the product to have, it's time to identify potential business risk. Risk appears when you only have assumptions about something (e.g., who the users are, what their needs are, and what functionality they're looking for). Once you see what will go into the product, you can identify the features and content that are risky. The risks here are that they will take too much time to design or develop and that you have no evidence that the users will actually use them. At this stage, you can apply UX research to validate these ideas.

UX research to apply

<u>User interviews</u>
User interviews give you insight into what the users need and what prior knowledge they may have on the product or problem. This insight will help you validate feature ideas and come up with new—and better—ones.

<u>Card sorting</u>
A great method for selecting which feature to keep and which to

discard is to do a card sorting exercise. To do this, you ask potential users to rank feature ideas based on how important they are to them. This way, you'll also learn how well they understand the described features.

Create a functionality map!

The tool I use all the time for organizing information is a functionality map. A functionality map is basically a mind map where we map out every functionality for the product. Pretty straightforward, right? The concept of mind mapping works extremely well, since you can start adding high-level features (e.g., Book a Lesson), then go deeper and add more and more data (e.g., *Sign Up, Choose a Location, Choose a Teacher*, etc.).

You can use various tools for creating mind maps, but I prefer to use XMind. It's free to get started, and it has all the functionality you need for this job. The goal is to collect every functionality and all the content you can think of that would be useful to have in the product. With XMind, you can also add symbols (e.g., colored flags) that can be used to indicate priority. You can use them to flag functions when you're unsure of user interest.

Try to map out the high-level ideas first. Don't jump into the details right away. This way, you'll have a clear overview of the project. Then, go deeper and add more details. For example, in our time zone app, we would add the "select time zones" as a high-level feature. Then, you can add that the product will know whether it's summer time or winter time in the given time zone, and the users can enter the desired location.

The goal of the functionality map is to have a great overview of the product and see what you have to design. It's up to you how much detail you want to put in the map. However, in my experience, it's best to go as deep as possible and list every detail you can think of at this stage. This is be-cause mind maps can handle and reflect an enormous amount of infor-mation without becoming overwhelming.

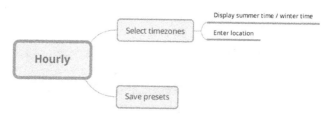

Building a functionality map will help you get a full picture of all the features you need to design.

Create a sitemap.

When you're working with a lot of screens, you need a tool that gives you an overview and helps you see which screens are related to each other. A simple tool for this is a sitemap. A sitemap displays the pages of a web-site and the logical relationship between them. It's a good idea to create a sitemap if you feel like you might get lost in the sea of information that's at your disposal. You can use sitemaps for keeping a record of the screens and content you've designed. This will help ensure that nothing is left out.

Sitemaps also help you decide what sort of content to put on which site—no designs here, just pure information architecture! And, sitemaps reveal how the navigation should work; in other words, which screens are acces-sible.

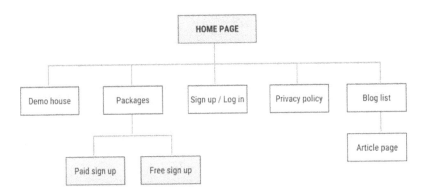

Creating a sitemap will help you keep track of all the screens you have to design.

User stories

If you know the agile method, user stories will be familiar to you. A user story is a one sentence statement about what the users want and why. They don't tell you how to design the solution. Instead, they focus on the user needs and force you to think through every process in the product.

Here's how it looks:

As a [type of user], I want to [...] so that [...].

For example:

As a product manager, I want to quickly find the right meeting time that works for everybody so that I don't have to waste time and energy organizing.

Why are user stories great?

- User stories will help you avoid dead ends in the product.
- User stories protect you from feature creep by focusing on user needs. Feature creep is when you keep adding feature after feature until the product becomes unusable.
- User stories make it simple and clear for everybody to know what each feature does and why it's important.

Step one: Start with "big-picture" stories (epics)

Take a look at the design brief (we'll get into this in greater detail later in this chapter), and and write out the big-picture stories for every function. Let's say you're designing a CRM. In this case, you have a lot of functions to manage users. You can come up with big-picture stories first:

"As a user, I want to quickly add a new lead to the CRM so that I can keep track of all information from now on."

As you can see, this is pretty general. It doesn't tell you what type of information to enter for a lead and how you can access the feature. At first, just write out these big-picture stories for the product.

Step two: Break down each story

Once you have your big-picture stories, you can break them down. The goal is to have a list of actionable stories that you can use to design an interface. Sticking with the CRM example, we can break that functionality down:

- "As a user, I want to access the add new lead feature so that I can quickly add new leads to the system."
- "As a user, I want to import existing data from an Excel sheet so that I don't have to manually re-enter all the information."
- "As a user, I want to save the entered data easily."

Step three: Add extra details to the stories

If you take a look at the second story, it's still not actionable because we didn't specify what kind of information we need to enter for a lead. This is when you add descriptions for the stories. In this case, I would add this:

- The user enters basic details:
- Name
- Upload profile picture (and remove or update)
- Email address
- Phone number
- LinkedIn URL
- Etc.

Now, this is something that you can sit down and start to flesh out, and that's exactly why we're creating stories!

Be flexible!

As you can see, I didn't use the "so that..." part all the time. It's great to indicate why that story is important for the users, but you don't always need to. For example, you don't have to give a reason why a user wants to log in or enter payment information; it's pretty straightforward, right? Likewise, in some cases, you just use the "As a user..." when speaking generally.

In other cases, you'll refer to a specific persona like, "As a product manager..." or "As a coffee fanatic..."

Think of user stories as a backlog for the design. With that said, it's best to start writing user stories before you start to design the screens. However, user stories constantly evolve throughout the process, so you have to update them. This is because you don't know all the stories up front. Despite a well-planned project, you still have a lot of things that will only come up during the design process—so keep those stories up to date!

Fire up an Excel sheet or use the User Stories template from the *7STEPUX® Resource Center.* Enter the big-picture stories, then continue to break them down, adding details until you have a great backlog that covers everything that needs to go into the design.

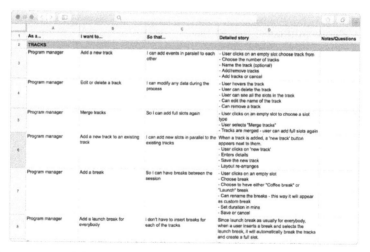

Create a spreadsheet for the user stories. This way, you can easily add new stories and more details.

Don't forget to update the stories! When designing the interfaces, if you add a new function or page, create a story for it. When you realize you've forgotten about an interaction, add it to the backlog immediately!

The Design Brief

So now that we understand who the users are, we have set goals for the project, collected feature ideas, and prioritized them. Since this information is distributed across several documents, we're going to create a short design brief that will serve as a starting point for the design. Let's not beat around the bush—a brief is meant to be brief! There's no need for a thousand-page-long SRS.

Sum up the most important things regarding the design.

- Who are the users?
- What are the user needs and goals?
- What are the product/business goals?
- What functions should we design?

Let's break it down.

1. Who are the users?

Sum up the most important points or ideas relating to your personas. The goal is that anyone who reads the design brief should be able to understand the different user types that need to be addressed with the designs. Don't go into too much detail! After all, that's what the user personas are for.

We have two different personas: (1) the product manager, who organizes global meetings on a weekly basis, and (2) the freelancer, who has an international clientele and who needs to organize meetings quickly, working across different time zones and maintaining a professional and organized approach to work.

2. What are the user needs and goals?

List the top needs/goals for the personas. These will be addressed during the design.

3. What are the product/business goals?

Dedicate a few sentences explaining what you want to achieve during the project. Be as specific as possible.

EXAMPLE:
Our goal is to increase user retention and bring users back frequently by finding new ways to engage with them on our website.

4. What functions should we design?

The most important part of the design brief is the functionality. All the other information is for adding context to the story. So, start to list and describe every function that goes into the product. If you did the functionality map, you just have to open it up, add the functions from there, and add a quick description.

Descriptions are very important. If you just write "book a lesson," that's not enough information. Everyone who reads the design brief should understand what the function does and how it works. If you skip this, there's a chance that you won't remember what the function or content was good for during the brainstorming session. The best way to describe the functions is to explain them through a story.

Returning to the time zone converter app, let's add and describe a function:

Function name:
Time picker

Description:
When a user enters the two desired locations (e.g., Budapest CET and Miami EDT), the time picker appears and displays two timelines. In the timeline, the user can see the usual work hours and the matching times highlighted in green. A slider will help the user pick the time that's good for both parties.

Key takeaways

- Planning is the most important part of the UX process. Don't rush it! Don't jump into the design straight away, as this will cause many headaches along the way.
- Start by collecting relevant information on the project from stakeholders, users, and any data that's available.
- Have a workshop with all the stakeholders present where you fill in the User-Centered Business Canvas, create the user personas (using the User Persona template), and brainstorm the functionality for the product. It's best to do one big workshop and get all these done as opposed to chopping them up into separate sessions.
- Learn how to create awesome UCBCs and user personas. These are invaluable tools that can ensure the product directions are clear and help you avoid confusion with stakeholders and clients.
- Do functionality maps to collect the high-level functions and pieces of content that need to go into the product. Then, use user stories to break these high-level functions down into a well-documented backlog for designers and developers to work from.
- Create a design brief and run it by every stakeholder to get a green light and make sure everybody is on the same page about what you want to achieve during the project.

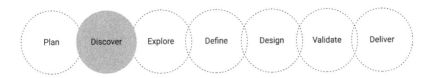

#2 Discover

Understand User Needs With UX Research

In the Discover phase, we're going to apply UX research to collect information and validate our assumptions regarding the users and the product. As I previously mentioned, the Plan and Discover phases are not strictly linear. Most of the time, they run in parallel to one another. Also, in some cases, you need to apply UX research or analytics straight away to understand the issues users face when dealing with an existing product. With that said, this chapter will serve as a toolkit. Whenever you have questions and need to collect more information, jump to this chapter and select a research method that will help you out.

Since there are many different research methods out there, it's vital to know when to apply a certain research type. Before you panic, you should know that these research methods are not that hard to execute; it's not rocket science. However, a lot of people use them in the wrong way or for the wrong purpose. For example, I've seen people doing usability tests to try to see if there's a real need for a product. Guess what? That's not what usability tests are for! Even worse, doing things this way could lead to false and misleading findings and bad product decisions later on.

To avoid this, when we discuss a method, we'll take a look at when to use it, what that method is good for, and what it's not good for. There are lots of techniques that are not included in this book, and there are many other methods out there that are also great. But I want to focus on the core research types that you can apply to a wide range of projects.

Research. Test. Measure. Analyze.

When I say "research," I can mean three different things.

UX research
UX research is for gathering information about the users, their problems, and the product. These are qualitative methods, and they can be used to understand underlying reasons, problems, and opinions. To put it simply, qualitative research tells us the "whys." The rule here is to "shut up and listen!" The methods include user interviews, observation, card sorting, and much more.

Tests
Tests help us validate a design or a product that we've built. Even though you will learn a lot about who the users are and what they want, the primary focus here is to test out an idea. Tests include usability tests, A/B tests, five-second tests, etc. This pretty much includes anything that has the word "test" in it somewhere. We'll explore these in detail in the Validate chapter.

Analytics

Have you heard about the build-measure-learn cycle? Well, you will in this book. Analytics and measurement are the cornerstones of product development. Analytics will tell you how the product performs. For example, if you say you want to optimize conversions, that's a measurement process. You set the initial value, the percentage of the conversion, do improvements on your website that you hope will boost conversions, and then measure the effect to see whether the new version is performing better or not. Analyzing data is a separate discipline; however, we can still learn a lot from using analytics in a smart way.

What can you expect from your UX research?

More and more companies realize that they can't make product decisions without feedback from the users. According to a study by Experience Dynamics, 73% of companies that are not currently conducting user experience testing will be doing so in the next 12 months. It's that vital! However, if you run into anyone who has doubts about UX research, just cite one of the reasons below to let them know why it's so essential.

With UX research you'll end up with fewer unnecessary features, and you can lower the cost of development. To put it simply, the primary goal of UX research is to build the product that users will want—not just something somebody thinks the users will love. If you build a product based on user feedback, you'll include all the necessary and useful features, functions, and content. This will save you a lot of headaches and unnecessary development rounds.

Your users will be happier and more engaged; they'll want to spend more time with the product. Research is not some obscure science! We can directly measure the impact of our product with research and tests. We want to make a product that's easy to use and engaging. UX research will tell us what we need to improve and why. A better product will mean that users will be more engaged with it. If you love something, you want to keep coming back to it.

You can also use the findings from UX research in other fields (e.g., in online marketing). Good UX will help bolster your SEO/SEM as well. In addition, it will help you run better ad campaigns—UX research provides lots of insights into who the users are, what they want, what their fears and goals are, and how you can reach them effectively.

My most important advice for doing research is to be "lean." You don't need expensive eye-tracking tech if you've never done any sort of research before. Don't jump in and blow all your money on research gadgets and gizmos. The more research you do, the better you'll become, and you'll know when you need to employ a certain research method. You'll also know if and when you need to involve a professional.

At the end of this chapter, you'll find a summary table of the research methods that we're going to cover in this book. Just remember, nothing is set in stone! The goal is to give you the information you need to design a kick-ass product! Doing a teeny-tiny bit of research is so much better than doing none at all. If you only have the time (or the budget) for a quick round of interviews, go ahead and do them! You'll learn a lot!

Recruiting test participants

I'm going to come right out and say it—recruiting test participants is a pain in the ass. This is like sweating away in a sauna so that you can jump into the cold water. You have to do it in order to get the benefits of user research. Because it's a pain in the ass, a lot of products and books tend to forget about recruiting, making it seem as simple as, "Just invite test participants," as if it were that easy.

Unfortunately, there's no easy solution to this problem (sometimes even throwing money at it will not help). This is why you need to plan ahead and build a tester database so that, over time, it will become easier to recruit people for your tests. Here's a rule of thumb: DON'T GIVE UP! Be smart and unleash your creativity. I'll help you as well!

How can you recruit test participants?

- Use your existing customer base.
- Recruit from potential users.
- Do remote testing with recruitment services.
- Guerrilla test with friends and colleagues.

Using your existing customer base

If you have an existing product, use the channels that you already have to recruit people. Basically, you can recruit two types of users. The first one is the potential user. They would use your product, but they haven't done so yet (maybe they only know the competitor's product). The second type of user is your existing customer.

You have to decide who to use in your test. You can learn different things from testing your existing customers versus testing new potential users. If you run a test with a potential user, you can measure first impressions, likes, and dislikes. This allows you to measure the overall first-time user experience. When you test with existing customers, they know their way around the product, so you can't measure the first-time experience, but you can get insight into the experience of a regular returning user. Here are a few cases when you need to do research on your existing customers:

Questions to address	Research methods
How are users using my product at the moment?	Observation
What do my customers think about my product?	User interviews
How should I build up the information architecture?	Card sorting
How can I improve the product to better serve returning users?	Usability test

How can I recruit existing customers?

Use your email list!

Did you build up an email list and collect subscribers? Great! Now it's time to use it to recruit test participants. Simply send out a nice email briefly explaining the research you're about to do and wait for participants to apply.

Reach out via social media!

Another great source for recruiting is social media. Do you have a Facebook page with thousands of followers? Put up a post! But it's not just about Facebook! You can successfully recruit people through Instagram and LinkedIn (mainly for B2B) as well. The trick is to make the post engaging. Explain why it's great if they apply, why their feedback is important to you, and how you'll use the feedback to create a better product for them.

Intercept visitors on your website.

You can put a nice pop-up on your website to attract visitors' attention and inform them that you're conducting user research. These are called intercept pop-ups because they capture the users in the middle of the process. There are dedicated solutions for this like Ethnio, but opting for a simple solution is also fine, such as a pop-up or tooltip that comes up when the user spends a bit of time on the page. If you have online chat support, you can use that to capture visitors and invite them for a test. Using these techniques, you can not only reel in your existing customers but also reach out and invite potential users.

Put a discreet pop-up on your website to tell the users that you're doing user research and that you need participants. Ask for their feedback and invite them to the test. You can offer them a gift card or downloadable content in return for their time, but a lot of people will participate for free.

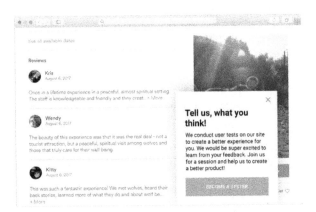

Place a small pop-up on your website to intercept visitors and recruit them for a user test.

Use customer support for recruiting.

There are a lot of people who write or call customer service because they have a question, some feedback, a problem, or some remarks. If you think about it, it's easier to involve somebody who has already decided to contact you and tell you about their problems or needs. They took the time, so it's important to them. There's a good chance that they'll be willing to participate and give you their feedback. Use customer support to reach out to your customers and invite them for a test. This is also a nice way to handle problems—if you have a problem and you realize that the company is trying to improve your experience and create a better product for you (via testing), you will love that company.

Recruiting potential users

Now this one is a bit trickier. Your existing customers will be loyal to you. They know and trust you, so a lot of them would be happy to come and talk to you about your product. But what about potential users? What's in it for them?

I see three reasons a potential user would accept your invitation. There could be more, but these are the most common reasons. The first reason is that people who experience a problem love to talk about it; it's human nature. If I'm concerned about something, and you ask me to discuss it with you, I probably will because it might help me find a solution for my problem. The second reason is that people want to appear smart. If you approach them stating that you need their expertise and opinion (and it doesn't sound like the usual marketing bullshit), a lot of people will be happy to help you.

And lastly, people are curious and user research is fun. I have recruited a lot of people who were just keen to try an interview or a usability test. You can build on that too. But the most important aspect is the problem. If the problem is valid and serious enough, you'll find people who want to complain about it, and that's exactly what you're looking for.

Use social media! Learn where everybody hangs out!
Again, one of the most powerful ways of recruiting people is to use social media. The trick is to find the platform that your potential users are actively using. It could be a Facebook group, a Twitter hashtag, a subreddit, a LinkedIn group, or any other little nook or cranny hidden away on a social platform. Invest some time in finding out where your users hang out.

Most of the time, Facebook works just fine. However, if you have a DIY product, I would advise you to check out Pinterest first, since this is a hot topic there and 89% of Pinterest users are female.

If I were to create a photo app, I would first take a look around on Instagram; there are even ads on Instagram that can be helpful for recruiting.

Leverage your friends, colleagues, and the rest of your personal network.
It's easy to recruit people from your personal network. This doesn't mean friends and family, but if you know more people than Mom and Dad, you have a chance of finding potential users in your network. Ask your colleagues and friends to help you out with recruiting and to introduce you to potential test participants.

Go to where they hang out.
What meetups and conferences do your users visit? Is there a place they frequently go? If so, this is a good way to capture them and even do a quick guerrilla test on the spot. For example, if my users are B2B and, let's say, designers, I would fire up Meetup, search for relevant UX or design meetups, go there, and collect leads to contact. Simple, right?

Recruit people through paid ads.

You can use Facebook, LinkedIn, or even Google Ads to recruit participants through paid ads. The success depends on how well you can target
the users. Although not a free option, paid ads allow you to reach more
people and collect more leads in a shorter time. I prefer platforms where I
can target my audience based on demographics (e.g., Facebook ads).

Pay testers on freelancing sites.

Okay, this should be at the end of your list, since I'm not a fan of paid
testing—simply put, I don't want there to be a bias. People are kind and
don't want to disappoint you, and in UX research, you really want the
harsh truth. However, you can find people on Mechanical Turk or Fiverr
who, for a few spare bucks, will do your tests. If you choose this option,
limit your tests to usability. Never try to validate a problem or idea with
this method. It's only good for finding out whether your product is usable or not.

Pay a recruiting agency.

This is a last resort, since it's quite pricey! However, paying a recruiting
agency can save you a lot of time and energy because you completely outsource the recruiting. Look for local recruitment agencies. They don't
have to be UX recruiters. For example, if you want to recruit developers,
there are a lot of IT recruitment companies who specialize in this. Before
you dive in, I recommend you check out ineedusers.com. This is the first
UX recruitment service run by UXers.

Do remote tests with recruitment services.

A lot of tests can be done remotely, and there are service platforms that
offer to do the test for you (including recruitment of test participants).
When we discuss a research or test type, we'll take a look at the remote
versions as well. Can they be done remotely? What are the benefits and
drawbacks of doing them remotely?

Here are a few remote testing platforms that will help you recruit test participants:

Test type	Service providers
Online usability testing	Usertesting.com, Whatusersdo, Userpeek
Card sorting	Optimal Workshop, UserZoom
Five-second tests, Click tests	UsabilityHub, Optimal Workshop, UserZoom

Do guerrilla tests with friends and colleagues.

There's also guerrilla testing. This is when you drop by a café and ask a few people to test your designs in exchange for a good cup of coffee. This is often called "hallway" testing. This is when you go out to a high foot traffic area and intercept visitors. If you don't have the time or the budget for a more formal way of testing, you can do guerrilla tests. But you need to know the limits first!

Guerrilla tests are only good for testing the usability of the product. A guerrilla test will give you a rough idea of what's usable and what's convenient in your product. It will also show you what is unusable and inconvenient and where the issues are. Simply go into a café or ask a few guys from your office building to take a look at your designs or product and test them out.

However, since your participants are not from your target audience, they can't be used to collect information on who the users will be and what they will need. They're not good for validating a product idea. Guerrilla tests are good for beginners who have never done any user research before. This type of test will act like a teaser for the more time-consuming research activities. Give it a shot, then continue with formal testing.

Build a participant database.

If you conducted a usability test and let the participant just walk away, that was money thrown down the toilet. Don't let them walk away until you've asked them if they'd be willing to come for another test later on. Wait, but if they already did a test, can I invite them again? Well, not for the same test, obviously, but there are lots of other options where you can reuse a candidate. If somebody has already done a test with you, it's likely that they'll do another one in the future.

With that said, there are multiple research types that go together nicely. For example, if you do interviews with a participant, you can invite them for a usability test next time. And when you go live with your product, their feedback is still valuable. Just think about how much energy you could save compared to letting them disappear and starting again from scratch.

So, anyone interested in taking part in a test should be put into a participant database, which is a simple spreadsheet to keep track of candidates. This is really helpful because people often cancel or are too busy to come, but later on you can reach out to them. Keep good track of anyone who is interested and don't forget to update!

If somebody is willing to participate in your tests, add them to the participant database. You can find a template for it in the *7STEPUX® Resource Center*. It's basically a simple spreadsheet where you can keep track of candidates who have applied for a test.

Later on, you just check this spreadsheet to see who you can invite for your next test.

Start recruiting now!

Set the criteria.
You need to set criteria so you'll know who to recruit for a test. It all comes down to your user personas. For example, the criteria can be that the user is a Facebook user, someone over 30, or someone who uses Twitter on a daily basis.

Define how you're going to decide whether somebody meets your criteria. Let's say you want to recruit active Twitter users who use the platform on a daily basis, not people who have Twitter but haven't logged in for a while. The benchmark would be users who post at least three times a day on Twitter. Now that's something measurable!

Write the screening questions!
When you recruit, you need a way to screen the participants to determine if they match the criteria you set. For this, you need a quick questionnaire that you can send out to candidates in order for them to submit their information. Google Forms is perfect for this. Keep it short and only ask for the necessary information (otherwise you risk losing prospects). Craft a compelling message that clearly describes the test itself and why the visitor should go ahead and apply.

Then, grab your criteria and transform it into screening questions. Be indirect and ask open-ended questions! Instead of asking if they use Twitter on a daily basis, ask how many times a day they tweet on Twitter.

Build the participant database!

Start to recruit test participants based on the list above. Anyone you make contact with should go into the participant database (use the template from the *7STEPUX® Resource Center*). Register their name and contact info and keep a record of what test they took part in. This way, you'll know who you can invite for the next test. At the end of each test, ask them if they will come again. If the answer is yes, make a note in the participant database!

User Interviews

User interviews are one of the most important techniques we have. You can do them the guerrilla way, in-house, or even outsource them to an agency, but it's hard to design a product without doing interviews with your users. The user interview is the bridge between you and your users. It will tell you who your users are, what they like and dislike, what they need, and what fears they may have. During the interview, we create a stress-free environment in which the participant feels relaxed and willing to share their thoughts.

User interviews help you understand the problems your users are facing. Interviews are a great way to discover what problems the users are experiencing. You'll gain insights into how they are currently solving the problem. You can examine what words they use to describe it, what fears are attached to it, and how they can be motivated.

If you're designing a new product, this is a must-have first step. You have a lot of assumptions about who the users are and what they need. With interviews, you will gain deep insight into these questions and validate your assumptions.

User interviews help you learn more about how your users think and look for information. Interviews can answer a lot of questions about how the users behave. How do they search for information? Who do they go to if they need information? What pages do they visit? Who influences their decisions? What existing solutions are they familiar with?

User interviews are not only useful for UX. The foundation of good marketing is that you know when, how, and what to talk to people about. You can create a communication strategy and messaging with the findings from the interviews. One of my favorite prompts for an interview is, "Tell me about the last time you did x." Through their response, you can learn a lot about how the user does something in practice and how they're currently solving their problems. You can use this information to come up with better functions and relevant content.

User interviews can help you find great new product ideas. Most products on the market are there because their creator had a problem. Somebody had a problem and built a solution to solve it. Later, they realized they weren't alone with this problem and proceeded to go to market with their solution. There's nothing wrong with discovering a product idea this way. By doing user interviews, you'll understand the real problems users face. Sometimes, you'll see stronger and more painful problems that are crying out for help. Doing interviews will help you see these problems and find great product ideas.

When it comes to interviews, the biggest challenge is in not leading users to provide the feedback you would like to hear. This is much harder than it might seem. During the interviews we're collecting data and validating assumptions, and there are things that you want to hear. Remember that people are very good at sniffing out what the other person wants to hear, and normally, we don't like to disappoint people.

Be skeptical!

Always be skeptical about what you hear during the interview. Always have that tiny voice in your head that's asking, *Did he say it because he feels this way, or does he just want to make me feel better?* Also, if somebody is uncertain on a topic, take it as a "no." You want solid information to validate your assumptions; it's dangerous to count on "maybe" or "probably."

Always avoid leading questions!

"Do you think this design is good?" This is a leading question that you must always avoid during an interview. You don't want to create bias in the research with questions that imply answers. Who would answer "no" to this question anyway?

Don't stop until you have enough information!

When you start doing interviews, it's tempting to cut them short after the first few participants give you great feedback. Though interviews are qualitative research and quantity is not what we're after, we still look for patterns between the interviewees. We have to make sure we're not getting isolated opinions and feedback. The simplest solution to this is to keep the sample size between 10 and 15 participants for an interview session. That will be enough feedback, and you'll see patterns.

How to use the findings of the interviews

Validate the user personas!

With interviews, you're collecting information that is featured in your user personas. You can learn about the problems and needs of your users. You can see the context of how they would use the product, and you can understand their fears and goals. Then, you can use these findings to update and refine the personas.

When you do this, you'll no longer have a made-up, fictive persona, but one that truly represents your users.

Validate and update the User-Centered Business Canvas!
The Problems section and the Users section are very important in the canvas. Interviews are a goldmine for validating and bringing new information to the canvas. Just like with the user personas, you might have a very fictive canvas at first, but with research, you can continuously update, refine, and make it viable.

Validate function and content ideas!
Since you'll learn about the needs of your users, you'll have the background to think about the features, functionality, and content they need. You can use this to validate existing functions or come up with new ones.

What interviews are not good for

You also have to know the limits of each research type. For example, during an interview, you shouldn't ask someone if they would use or buy the product. If you were to do so, it would lead to false results. If I ask you if you would buy a product, you might say, "Well, yes, maybe." Or, "Hell, yeah, it's great!" But this is all hypothetical. And again, people don't like to disappoint other people. Most people are kind and polite in a situation like this and will tell you what you want to hear.

Also, interviews are not good for validating design solutions. For example, please don't drive your participants nuts by asking them whether you should use blue or green for a button color. Don't use interviews to collect feedback on the designs!

Remote versus in-person interviews

The best way to do interviews is in person. By doing this, you'll meet your customers, see how they look, see how they dress, and see what gadgets they have. You'll also learn how they communicate and see their gestures and expressions, which will help you interpret their thoughts and feelings better.

When doing in-person interviews, you generally have more time; if somebody takes the time to meet you, chances are they won't vanish after 20 minutes. From a validation standpoint, it's a good sign if you can get people to meet with you and discuss a problem; this means it's interesting to them or that they are serious about finding a solution.

So, live interviews are great. But sometimes you just can't do them. Maybe it would take too much time to organize the in-person interviews. Maybe the users are geographically distributed, or maybe you just don't have the budget for in-person interviews. If this is the case, don't worry. You can still get very good results conducting the interviews over the phone or via Skype (or with a similar tool).

The upside of conducting remote interviews is that you can recruit faster and set up more interviews in less time. In addition, most people are busy (especially if you're targeting B2B), so they would be better off with a call than an in-person meeting. The downside is that you can't see people's gestures, and it takes practice to learn how to conduct good interviews over the phone.

Start doing interviews!

Recruit interviewees.

Find 10 to 15 people who fit your target audience. Aim for a 20-minute to 40-minute-long interview. Sometimes it will be more than that, but don't scare people away by asking for too much of their time. People will invest 20 minutes, and if they're interested, they won't hang up when the time is up.

Set goals and define your questions.

To get the most out of your interviews, set some goals and define your questions first. You want to answer these questions and validate assumptions using the interviews. Always do this, because without having set questions, you'll just end up with a lot of data that you won't know what to do with it.

Example of a good goal:
We want to find out why our users don't want to make a purchase when using a mobile device.

Example of a good question (for yourself):
What information are they looking for when they browse to buy a house?

Example of a good assumption:
We think it's difficult for website owners to understand web analytics.

Craft the questions that you'll ask the participants.

Use open-ended questions like, "Tell me about the last time you did x." Kill the leading questions! For example, don't ask, "Do you find it difficult to understand web analytics?" This is a yes/no question that will bias the interview. As a rule of thumb, if you can answer a question with a yes or no, it's a leading question. Got it? Now, *that* was a leading question.

Make the interviewee feel comfortable and relaxed.

Ensure that your participants feel comfortable and relaxed. You don't want them to be stressed out. Take notes, but don't overdo it. Ask for permission to record the interviews so you can pay more attention to the interviewees and not your notes. While doing the interviews, focus on their gestures and look for emotions (both positive and negative).

Analyze the findings and implement them.

After an interview, sit down and see how the findings correlate to your questions, assumptions, and hypothesis. Be critical! Be especially critical toward things that validate your assumptions. Always consider whether the users have given you their honest opinion or were just trying to make you happy. Remember, people are good at sniffing out what you want to hear.

Observation

Henry Ford once said that if he asked his clients what they wanted, they answered that they wanted a faster horse. At this point, Ford could have said, "Okay, so now I know what the user needs." The task is clear: breed better, faster horses. In this case, every farmer today would be keen to have Ford horses, but we wouldn't have affordable automobiles.

Obviously, Ford didn't go that way. Instead of focusing on what people said they wanted, he observed them and focused on what they needed. He knew that the real problem was that people needed a faster way to get from A to B and to spend less time traveling.

I've got good news for you. This is something that you can also—and should—do. To understand real user needs, you have to observe what problems your users are experiencing and how they're solving those problems right now. It's pretty basic; just think about how much easier it is to see and solve other people's problems compared to solving your own.

Observation is also known as customer visits or field studies. During the observation, we're focusing on what the users are doing instead of focusing on what they're telling us. This is extremely useful when you're dealing with a very practical problem that people are experiencing on a daily basis. For example, if I were to ask you how you use Facebook or Google, it would be a difficult question to answer because you do it almost instinctively, which makes it hard to recall. So, instead of asking a question, I would ask you to show me how you do it. This will give me a lot of valuable insight.

There's one more thing you have to know about people. When you learn how to do something for the first time, you just struggle your way through it. Most of us do not solve problems scientifically, we just jump in and try to find a solution. And, once we managed to do something once, we don't look for another solution.

It's just not in our nature to constantly look for ways to improve something that we can already do. The funny thing is that it might be a time-consuming, tiring, or dumb way to do it, but this is how we operate. You can uncover these problems with time-consuming, repetitive tasks by observing users.

How does observation work?

During an observation, you sit down with your users and ask them to show you how they perform a task or how they solve a problem. It's important that you do this on-site, in the field. You have to understand the context and see the environment where the users are facing the problem and using existing solutions.

If I were to redesign an existing piece of software, I would sit down with the users and ask them to show me how they're using the software right now. This is not a usability test; I'm not measuring the success of the task. Instead, I'm trying to learn how they're using the product.

- What features are they using?
- How are they interacting with them?
- What obstacles are they facing?
- What are the repetitive, time-consuming ways they're using to solve their problems?
- What existing solutions are they using to solve their problems?

Compared to usability tests, there are no tasks during an observation. This allows you to get a better sense of what people are using and how they're using it. It's pretty basic. If you ask your users to find and use a feature during a usability test, they might find it and find out how to use it. But, it's possible that, on their own, they wouldn't find it or wouldn't use it because it's not convenient.

When to use observation

As a rule of thumb, I would say that if you want to find out how people are using a product now, or you want to see how they're using existing solutions (even the competitor's products), then it's time for some observation. Use observation if you want to understand how people are doing something practical. In this case, interviews are not the best tool because we can't rely on the participants' memories. For example, if I want to understand the reading habits of people at a library, I would use interviews.

104

If I want to find out how people are using the automatic rental machines in the library hall, I would conduct an observation.

So, what can you use observation for? Here are a few things:

- To see and understand the current, existing solutions people are using
- To observe how they're using the product
- To get new feature ideas and even new product ideas based on real user needs
- To learn the users' language—what jargon they use, what they know, and what they don't know
- To identify their usual behaviors and the workflows they use
- To understand the real user needs

THINK OF HENRY FORD! Rely on what you see and observe. Look for problems and user needs. Look for time-consuming and repetitive tasks, dumb solutions, and problems. These are the real problems that you have to solve.

If you already have a product...

If you already have a product and you want to find out how users are using your product now, you have to ask a few of your existing clients to show you how they're using the product. When doing an observation, make sure the user is using the product where they would naturally do so—if it's in the kitchen, observe them in the kitchen. If it's on the street, go out and do your observation there. The location and the context have a huge impact on how we use something. If you're in a shop using an app, you might be distracted and unable to give it your full attention.

It's a completely different context when you're in a café—a relaxed environment—having a nice cappuccino, and reading the news.

Go ahead and recruit eight participants and ask them to show you how they're using your product. What features are they using? What difficulties are they facing? You can also ask the same questions that you would during an interview. In their natural environment, people can more easily recall how they perform their tasks.

If you don't have a product...

You don't have to have a product to conduct an observation. You can simply do an observation to discover what current solutions the users have at their disposal. You can also test out competitors' products to learn what's good and what's bad about them. You'll need to recruit eight potential users and ask them to show you how they're solving problems right now. Visit them and learn about their environment and needs. This way, you can validate your feature ideas and also validate your assumptions about the users, then you can come up with better ideas.

You can test out the competitors' products as well. For example, if you're designing an analytics tool, you can test the current solutions that your users are already aware of (like Google Analytics, or maybe Mixpanel). To design a better payment system, check out Stripe and PayPal and look for room for improvement.

Card Sorting

We talked about information architecture during the Plan phase. In essence, this means asking what information has to be put where and what the hierarchy is. There can be a lot of questions about what information is important for the users and where to put that information so they can find it. A great exercise to learn how people organize information is known as card sorting.

Below, we're going to cover four card sorting techniques. The idea is pretty basic. You take cards (like Post-its) and write information on them. Then, you ask your test participants to group the cards based on what looks logical to them. One way we can use this technique is to learn how to build up the navigation so it will be convenient and straightforward for the users.

Method 1: Open card sort

The simplest method is to leave the cards unsorted. Create a bunch of cards, write labels on them, and lay them on the table. Then, invite the users to identify the cards (explain what they're able to make of them) and group them logically. Once they're ready, ask them to name the groups. For example, you would write out every element from your website navigation on the cards. After this, you would ask the users to create categories and name them.

This method is great to learn how users group information. Since they have to name the groups, you can learn a lot about what jargon and expressions they use. Based on this, you can come up with better copy and wording of functions and navigational elements.

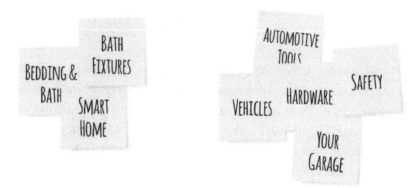

Open card sort—a great way to learn how users group information.

Open card sort gives extremely valuable help when building up your navigation. Designers and stakeholders tend to build up navigation (e.g., the product categories on an e-commerce site) based on what seems logical to them; however, it's not often logical and convenient for the users. Many times, users look for information in an entirely different place than you would expect. This is why it's important to learn what's logical to them and where they would put the information.

An open card sort is best to do at the beginning of the process when you're designing the information architecture. For example, if you're designing (or redesigning) an e-commerce site, doing an open card sort is a great start to understanding how people would build up the product categories. You can instantly use this information to build better navigation.

Method 2: Closed card sort

When you perform a closed card sort, you give the users predefined groups, and they have to place the cards in the groups. This is a great method to see how users place information within an existing structure.

Returning to the e-commerce example, you can use a closed card sort to find out which product category people would place each product in.

Closed card sort. Use this technique to find out how users would place information within an existing structure.

Method 3: Reversed card sort or tree testing

Take the idea of grouping the information and reverse it. We take an existing information architecture and ask the user to find information in the structure. This is often called "tree testing" because a website is usually organized in a hierarchy of topics and subtopics—like a tree. For example, you show the users the navigation of the e-commerce site. Then, you give tasks like, "Please show me how you would find product X."

Tree testing in OptimalSort.

During the analysis, you're evaluating how fast users find the information, which route they take to find it, where they get lost, and which path they take instead. So, doing tree tests will help validate how good the structure is that you've designed.

An important note here:
The structure is based on two things: (1) the placement of the information and (2) the wording. The structure could be great, but the users might not understand the function or navigation due to the wording. Card sorting and tree testing help test the wording.

Method 4: Ranking cards

You can also use cards to rank information. For example, you can create cards for all the functionality you have (or plan to have in the product). Create a few groups like "important," "not really important," and "not important at all." Then, ask users to identify each function (so you can check whether they understand what the function does) and put them in a group. You can also give the cards to the users and ask them to rank them from "not important" to "important" (vertically or horizontally).

Ranking cards—ask users to group cards based on how important are they to them.

You should apply ruthless prioritization when it comes to functionality. You have limited resources and time, so you want to make sure you only deal with functionality that's important to the users. Doing a card rank is a good way to eliminate useless functions.

You can also use this technique to prioritize the content. Imagine that you have a website. On the website, you only want to show the crucial information (since you have little time to convince visitors to stay on your site). Create cards and write all the information that you plan to feature on the website or page (e.g., on your main page). Then, ask the users to rank the information based on how important it is to them.

What can you use card sorting for?

Card sorting will show you how users are grouping information.
Finding information quickly as compared to wandering through a website looking for something make for two very different experiences. The goal is to have an information architecture that reflects the needs of the users. Card sorting will help you learn about how people organize and find information. You can directly implement the findings to improve the navigation.

Tree testing will show you how users search for information.
With tree testing, you can test out the navigation of a website. Ask yourself, *Can people find what they're looking for? Can they find it quickly enough?* If not, *Where do they get lost? What can be misleading to users?*

Ranking cards will help you prioritize functions and content based on user feedback.
It's extremely valuable to know which features are important to the users. Obviously, you don't want to build a feature that won't be used later—that would be time and energy wasted. Use card sorting to find out what's crucial to the users—what they can't live without.

When it comes to mobile design, the biggest limitation is the space available. Compared to the desktop screen, you have very limited space on a mobile screen. Therefore, you must find out which functions are the most important and which features should be accessible right away. Ranking is a simple tool to help you prioritize better and make clearer decisions.

You'll learn a lot about wording.

One of the most important aspects of UX is wording. But, oftentimes, this is the most overlooked aspect. In many cases, simply changing the wording can have a serious impact on the overall user experience—in turn, the whole experience is improved.

When it comes to card sorting, we work with text instead of visual designs. This gives us the opportunity to test out our copy and wording. Are the names of the functions straightforward enough that people can understand them? Do they know what each function does based on the name or description? Do they understand the jargon being used?

The bottom line is, you need to make sure that people understand what's written on each card. Be aware that if they don't understand something, they might not tell you. This is why you have to ask them to identify each card and explain what they think that card represents. Otherwise, you won't know whether they placed a card in a specific group because they understood it or because they had no idea and didn't want to appear stupid.

You can also use a card sort just for the wording. For example, if you're not sure about the jargon the users are familiar with, do a closed card sort. The group names should be a description of the expression or jargon. The cards should represent possible expressions. Ask the users to pair the descriptions with the best matching expression. Look for patterns. If a lot of people pair an expression with a description, that's supporting evidence.

Card sorting is not just for navigation.

Now comes creativity! A lot of people think of card sorting as just an exercise to build better navigation. I once followed the same path, so I know. But there's more to card sorting than just navigation.

Here are a few areas where card sorting excels:

- Testing wording and jargon
- Ranking functionality
- Creating a bonus system. What prize or achievement is important to users? This is a great help when creating gamified products; you have to understand what users think about the benefits and what makes achievements attractive to them.
- Discovering emotions and feelings. What words do they use to describe the brand, function, or piece of content?
- Using images. For example, if you want to learn what words and emotions users connect with an image, use a card sort. This is a great help when designing a landing page.
- Prioritizing content. What information should go where? Card sorting is a great tool to help you out with arranging information, such as determining what content to put on the main page.

In-person versus remote

The benefit of in-person card sorting is that you can ask people to identify the cards and tell you what they think about them. Why did they put a card in a certain group? Why do they think that feature is the most important one? On the other hand, remote card sorting will give you a bigger sample size and be more accurate. It also costs less and can be done faster than organizing in-person sessions. The interesting thing about card sorting is that it's both qualitative and quantitative at the same time. Doing an in-person card sorting with 10 to 15 participants will mainly be qualitative. However, doing remote tree testing with hundreds or even thousands of participants will give you a decent amount of quantitative feedback.

So, it's best to do is both. Start with an in-person card sort to understand how people think and get a better understanding of the "whys." When you start to see patterns, go remote with a bigger sample size. This will help prove that the findings were not isolated cases.

Tools for the trade

To do an in-person card sort exercise, you just need some Post-its and Sharpies. But, for a tree test and a remote card sort, you need an online tool. Here are a few good ones to start with:

OptimalSort
This is one of the best tools for card sorting; it's easy to use and will help you analyze the results. OptimalSort also provides great user support. It's powered by Optimal Workshop, which is a company that runs multiple tools for UX research. We'll talk more about them in the Validate chapter.

UserZoom
This is a complex UX research platform that offers card sorting and tree testing. UserZoom also provides usability testing, surveys, and testing for mobile devices.

Start doing a card sort!

Decide what method you need.
If you want to collect information and see how people organize data, do an open sort. If you have an existing structure and you want to see where to place new information, do a closed sort. If you want to test if users can easily find the information they're looking for, go with the tree testing method. If you want to know which features to build and what information is relevant for the users, do a ranking.

Decide if it should be done in person or remotely.
If you have the opportunity, go in person first. Then, when you start to see patterns, do a remote card sort—which will give you more accurate results.

Prepare the test.
Create the cards and define the groups (if you're doing a closed sort). For a tree test, you have to build up the structure (e.g., add topics, then sub-topics). It's worthwhile to limit the cards in a session to between 20 and 30; otherwise, things can become overwhelming.

Invite the participants.
For an in-person test, invite 10 to 15 participants. You're basically good to go at 10 or more. If done remotely, invite 30 to 40 participants for a session. You can have more, but it's better to do multiple rounds first to improve and iterate between the rounds. The outcome we're looking for is to find patterns. It's possible that you're going to see patterns after 10 participants. But in some cases, you'll need a bigger sample size. If you've done multiple rounds with 30 to 40 participants and still don't see patterns, either the test was too vague or the task was not straightforward enough.

Think-aloud protocol (in-person card sort only).

If you're doing an in-person card sort, ask the participants to express their thoughts and feelings out loud. Identify what each card represents and have them interpret it for you. This will help you identify wording issues. Then, have the participants give a reason as to why they placed a card in a certain spot.

Analyze the results.

When analyzing the results, look for patterns. If you're doing an open sort, examine the cards that were frequently grouped together and find out if there are patterns between the naming of the groups as well. In a closed sort, look for cards that are frequently put in a certain group. The more that happens, the more evidence there is to suggest a pattern.

Here are a few additional things to look for:

- Which cards do users find confusing or difficult to place in a category?
- Were there any ideas for new cards?
- Was the wording clear?

Analytics

Obviously, to think data informed, you need data. Data can come from interviews and usability tests—this is qualitative data that helps us understand the "whys" and how people think. And, of course, we have numbers as well—this is the quantitative side. The numbers will tell you how the product performs and will make the whole process measurable. Numbers will tell you if you reached your goals. But, to analyze data, you need to find a way to collect it. A basic example is setting up Google Analytics and letting the data come to you.

We're going to cover a few methods on how data can help design a better user experience. My goal is to show you how to use analytics and how to insert it into your process. It's not my job to go into nitty-gritty detail—there are some great books and resources for that, and I'll recommend a few in the last chapter. Understanding and excelling in analytics is a long journey, and you have to know the basics first.

Before we dive in, let me give you the simplest and smartest advice I've ever received in my career. The biggest pitfall when it comes to analytics is to jump in and collect data without having questions and setting goals first. It's easy to get excited about the latest analytics tools because they're fancy and can show everything you need for your job. But without questions and goals, you'll end up not knowing how to interpret the data and how to use it to design better products—it will simply end up in a report to be forgotten.

It's like going to a supermarket without a list of ingredients and things you need to buy for dinner. You're just throwing random stuff into your shopping cart. How likely is it that you'll have everything you need for dinner?

The solution is a no-brainer. Always have clear goals when collecting data. If you fail to set goals, you won't know how to use the data. From the UX perspective, we can have four types of goals:

- Make the process measurable
- Find problems to be solved with UX expertise
- Support qualitative research
- Validate assumptions about users and the product

Make the process measurable.

Analytics make product performance and goal achievement measurable. Taking a look at how many users you have, how much time they spend on your pages, and conversion rates are considered measurement. Measurement shows us whether we've reached the product and business goals. Measurement plays a crucial role in product design. When you want to improve an existing product, you have to understand how it performs; you need to be able to identify what needs to be worked on. Analytics will make the process measurable because after you make the changes to the product, you can compare the numbers with the previous data. Measurement is good for

- understanding how the product currently performs,
- seeing if the changes we made to the product were successful, and
- making product design measurable.

Find problems to be solved with UX expertise.

As UXers, we use analytics to dig for problems in the product. Quantitative data can tell us "where" the problem is, but most of the time, it won't tell us "why" there's a problem. For example, analytics can help you identify the pages with high bounce rates. You know that there's a problem causing people to abandon that product page, but you don't know why. What changed their minds? Is there a technical issue? Could they not find the information they were looking for? Is it a usability issue? Or, is it just that a rainbow pony kept popping up in the middle of the screen? To answer these questions, we need to apply qualitative research (interviews, observation, etc.). Analytics is used to locate the problem.

Here are a few examples of how you can use analytics to uncover problems:

- Identify which traffic sources your visitors are coming from. This may bring up a lot of questions. For example, why is the conversion rate lower with users on mobile devices? Why is the retention lower among users coming from Facebook?
- Identify technical issues such as slow page load times, dead URLs, and so on. Developers usually log these issues when they encounter them. It's good practice to check those lists to avoid technical issues.
- Create a funnel that the visitor must go through to become a customer. At which stage in the process do they abandon the product? Where do they spend too much time?

When you see where the problem is, take the next step and apply qualitative research to understand why the problem exists so you can come up with solutions. Be patient with yourself; it takes time and practice to be good at finding flaws in the process and locating problems by using analytics.

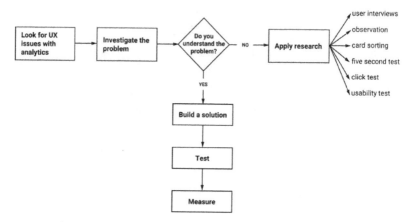

The process of localizing a problem that needs to be solved.

Support qualitative research with data.

Let's turn things around. Another smart way to use data is to support qualitative research. Let's take a usability test as an example. A usability test consists of five participants. They sit down and perform a few tasks with your product while you observe them. You're looking for errors, where the participants get lost or frustrated, in order to learn how to improve the product.

Usually, a task can be carried out in several ways. Let's say we do a usability test on booking.com. The task is to book a hotel and carry out the whole booking process. Now this can be done several ways. Different users will focus on different things. For example, some people might use the search panel; other people might choose to browse popular destinations. You'll be able to observe a lot of different user behaviors. Sometimes you might see something interesting, but you'll find out that it's not significant because you only have feedback from one or two participants.

When this happens, you can apply analytics tools to see if there's a pattern or if it is an isolated case.

For example, when you design a checkout process, you should streamline the process and make it simple for users. During a usability test, you'll learn if users are comfortable entering their data or if they don't trust the product. It might turn out that you ask for too much information or that the lack of an SSL drives them away. More and more people are now aware that they have to check for the small green padlock at the top left corner. Also, modern browsers have started to warn users of potential issues with a website's security. When you see something like this in a usability test, you can check the analytics to see if it was a one-time issue or a more general problem. Check to see how many people abandon the checkout from that specific location.

Fuel the design process with data.

The third goal of analytics is to fuel the design process with data. During planning, we had a lot of assumptions about the users, the business, and functionality as well. We can use analytics to validate our assumptions. Of course, you have to have a product to have analytics. When you have the product, you can use analytics from the very start.

- Use current analytics (demographics, behavior, devices used, etc.) to build out the user personas.
- When designing the user journey and seeing what routes the users take, you can see how they are currently using the product.

There are new players entering the analytics market every month. Analytics tools are getting smarter and smarter at collecting every possible piece of data from users. I just want to give you a few ideas of what tools you can use; you take the next step—there's a wide range of tools available for all purposes. For example, there are mobile-specific analytics tools like Appsee or Flurry.

Google Analytics

We can't leave Google Analytics off the list. It's free, and it pretty much collects all the data you might need and offers a lot of integration with other tools as well. These features make Google Analytics the most used analytics tool. Most of the examples in this chapter can be done with Google Analytics. The downside is that it's pretty difficult to understand the interface. You also have to get your hands dirty and really dig for useful and meaningful data. This is why 90% of Google Analytics users only use it to monitor their page views.

Mixpanel

Mixpanel is just one of the event-based analytics tools out there. They think in reverse. It's not about collecting all the information and then digging into it. Instead, you can define events to be tracked and set up funnels (e.g., the steps a user has to take to purchase an item). An event can be clicking on a button, filling in an input, and/or any other interaction the user can perform inside the product. Basically, you tell the tool what the users can do with the product, then the tool will show you where people abandon the process and where the problems are in the funnel.

Visual analytics

From a UX standpoint, we have to dedicate a separate chapter to visual analytics. With these tools, we can gain insight into what users are doing inside the product and see it visually. Heatmaps, scroll maps, and video session recordings are all visual analytics.

These tools can help us better understand the behavior of the users. Also, they are much faster and cheaper than doing UX research like usability tests or interviews. These tools can be your best bet when you don't have enough traffic for doing A/B tests.

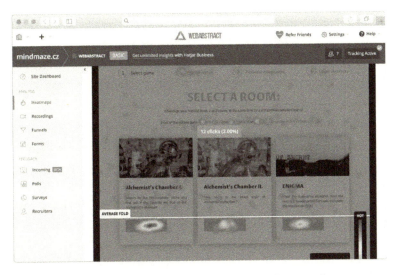

Hotjar offers a wide range of visual analytics tools.

Heatmaps and scroll maps

To put it simply, heatmaps record every user click and display them visually. The more users click on one spot, the "hotter" it gets (typically, a small number of clicks will be represented by cold blue colors and move to hot red).

Scroll maps work the same way, but instead of clicks, they show you how far users scrolled down on a page. The more they scrolled down, the hotter it appears. These tools also show you the above the fold area–what the average users see on your website without scrolling at all.

What can a heatmap tell you?

- It can help you understand what's important to users. This will help you make sure that your priorities are in the right place. You'll be able to tell if they don't see or don't pay attention to content.
- This might surprise you, but many times people click on unclickable places. For example, they click on a headline or on something that looks like a button. This is crucial information for us. Why did they click on that? What did they want or expect? What made them think it was clickable? Maybe an element in the design is misleading, or maybe they missed the information and thought that if they clicked, they would learn more about it.
- By analyzing a heatmap, it will become clear to you what draws the users' attention and what doesn't. You can use this information to make sure that users encounter the important elements on the page.
- By analyzing clicks and mouse flow (e.g., on a checkout page) you can understand where people might face difficulties and where they give up in the process.

When should you use a heatmap?

- To find answers to questions like, "Do the users click on this?"
- To show you if important information is in the right place. Heatmaps and scroll maps will show you if people pay attention to something or not. Use this to make sure they can easily see and find information that you want them to find.
- To identify whether something is missing from a page. If people spend a lot of time on a page scrolling back and forth, but there are just a few clicks, that's a strong sign that they're looking for something that they can't find (or they can't find fast enough).

This behavior can also indicate that something is holding them back from taking the next step.

Video recordings

There are tools that record a video showing what the users are doing on your website. They record every user session so you can sit down and watch. This is a huge opportunity, since this way you can see what they're doing with your product in a real and non-moderated environment. You can see how they move their mouse, how they scroll, where they click, and what they type in.

- What questions can video recordings answer, and what information can they reveal?
- What does the user journey look like? How do users browse your website, and what pages do they visit?
- What does a session look like? How long does it last? How do returning users behave?
- Where are the usability issues (where do people get lost, where do they get frustrated, and where do they make errors)?
- Are the users missing any information?

Okay, I know it all sounds great. But, when I tell this to people, most of them say, "I want it now!" Then they sit down, start watching the recordings, and realize that they have no idea what to do with the information. This is what happens if you start to use this tool without a purpose or goal. To avoid this, I recommend two ways of using video recordings.

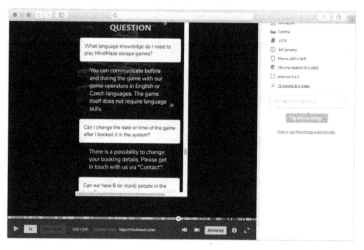

Video session recordings in Hotjar.

Use video recordings to explore problems.

When you run into a usability issue—or any other problem—you can use videos to observe where users run into problems. For example, by looking at analytics, you can see that something is going wrong on your cart page because there are too many people abandoning the cart after they land on that page. What ungrateful users, right? Sit down and start watching videos of your users interacting with the cart page. What happens? What do they do? What's not clear to them? Where do they click? Where do they try to click (is it not clickable?). Where do they get stuck in the process?

Use video recordings to fuel qualitative research with more data.

The other great way to use session recordings is to back up qualitative research. Maybe you see something interesting on a usability test, but you're not sure whether it's a common pattern or issue. Simply go ahead and look for similar behaviors on the videos. For example, while usability testing a checkout page for an e-commerce site, you might notice that two of the participants found it annoying that the "next" button was placed on the right side. This is a crucial observation. The navigation has to be convenient and clear. But you need more proof, because this could be an isolated case. By looking at the videos, you can hunt for the same pattern. If that button isn't in the right place, you'll see signs in the clicks and the mouse flow; for example, people almost clicking on a wrong button, moving their mouse back and forth at the wrong area, or not finding the "next" button quickly enough.

Tools of the trade

Hotjar:
When Hotjar launched, they collected every tool necessary for visual analytics into one product. Before Hotjar, you had to pay for several different tools to get everything. One tool was to create heatmaps. Another tool could record the videos. A third one was great to create polls and surveys to collect more data. Then Hotjar came in, put it all together in one product, and now offers it for a nice price. I'm an early adopter of the product, following up with them since they were in beta. They had multiple rounds of funding, but they're still looking out for what the customers (we) want.

Fullstory:
FullStory records every session as video and tracks every event automatically. This means that you have a conversion funnel where you can see how many users completed the process or bounced, and you can go into each step and see the relevant video recordings. Thanks to this advanced filtering, you can ask complex questions and find the answers in a video.

You can find answers to questions like, "What are my customers doing?" And, "Who came from a mobile device and spent over three minutes on the site but didn't convert?" FullStory can also sync with your user base so you can identify and create segments for your existing customers. Not sure what this means? Just imagine that you can identify what first-time users are doing and what your returning visitors are doing inside your product.

Smartlook:
Smartlook is the honorable mention here. Like the two mentioned above, it also records every session on video. It's a good tool to start with—it records 1,500 sessions/month for free, making it a pretty good starter package.

UX surveys

We also have to talk about collecting the feedback from the users. Interviews will help you a lot in understanding your users and their goals. Using observation will lead to better solutions. But there are other techniques which bring valuable insight and help you to learn more about your users.

When you create a survey, you specify a couple of questions that you send to the users (e.g., via social media or an email list). Participants answer the questions and give their opinions. This might be the most used tool in UX and marketing. It's fast, easy to create, and works online—so you can reach more people with less effort.

But before we stamp the "best UX tool ever" on surveys, we must understand their limits. One limit to surveys, and this one's a biggie, is that they're unmoderated. This means we have no control over the events.

128

Moreover, we only see the answers of the participants—no facial expressions, gestures, emotions, or reactions. And, since surveys are done online, we have less time to get information. Most people are willing to tell you their opinion at length in person, but they're not so willing to type in hundreds of characters to help you. There are two cases when you need a UX survey:

- You can't do any interviews, observations, or usability tests—not even remotely
- You want to back up your research findings with more data

You can't do any interviews, observations, or usability tests

Maybe you can't do any of these research methods because you don't have the time or the budget or the users are too busy and widely geographically distributed. If you don't have the opportunity to do them remotely, a UX survey can be helpful. A few questions that a good UX survey can answer:

- Who are the users? What are the user needs?
- What do the users think about my brand? What do they think about my product? What do they think about a single feature?
- What do the users purchase? Why?

You want to back up your research findings with more data

The best way to use UX surveys is to back up your qualitative research findings with more data. For example, you saw something interesting during the observation or in the interviews, and you want to find out if it's a pattern among the target users. Surveys allow for larger sample sizes. This is what surveys are best for!

Interviews and observation will give you insight as to what the users need, think, and feel. When you see something interesting and have questions, use surveys to validate your findings. Whenever you feel that it would be great to see if other users are thinking the same thing, you know you need to use surveys!

How to get started with UX surveys

Decide what you want to learn first.

Do you have a question that you want to get answered? Did you notice something during the interviews and want to find out if other users think the same way? What are the things that you don't know about the users and the product? What are the risky assumptions that you need to collect information about?

Focus.

Don't create a thousand-page-long survey. Nobody will fill it out. Focus on the core questions, and only ask for information that is absolutely necessary. If you have too many questions, it's better to break things down into multiple surveys.

Come up with screening questions.

Narrow it down and specify who you need to answer your questions. Also, determine whose opinion is not relevant at that moment. Always add screening questions to the survey. These questions will help you sort out the useful answers that are relevant to the project. If you don't remember how to create screening questions, go back to the section where we covered recruiting.

Decide how the participants will find the survey.

If you're building an email list of users, it will come in handy here. But if you aren't, just relax, you still have multiple options. If you have an existing product, consider placing an element that drives the visitors' attention to the survey. Also, look up where your target users hang out (e.g., social media). Groups and forums where you can post your survey work especially well. If you follow this practice, be nice and proactive. Don't just toss in a link to the survey. Describe why it's important to you and why you're counting on the members of the group. Be human! People will be likely to help you if they feel you're personally asking for their help.

Tools of the trade

Google forms:
This tool is easy to use, free, and it works just fine. When you've created your survey, you'll get a link that you can share.

Typeform:
Typeform has a different take on surveys. Instead of showing every question at once, they take the visitor by the hand and walk them through each question, one by one, on a clean and beautiful interface. Also, apart from the standard elements of a survey, Typeform offers a lot of creative ways to ask for information. Without a doubt, this improves the UX of surveying.

Surveymonkey:
SurveyMonkey is a complex surveying tool with several templates and support for team collaboration. You can even use videos in the survey. SurveyMonkey also has a paid service for recruiting participants from all over the world.

Get instant feedback with polls

Polls are micro-questionnaires that usually pop up in the bottom right corner on a website. They ask for pieces of information, then they disappear. Polls offer exciting opportunities—giving the ability to intercept visitors at a certain page or time or in the middle of a process. Just think about it! Your users are on your site searching for information they can't find; a poll appears asking, "What information is missing?" Or, when they're browsing the pricing page but not taking the next step, you can ask, "What's holding you back from signing up?" We can use polls to look inside people's heads when they're using our product or browsing our site.

Inside a poll, you can put a single line or long-text answer, give options for the users to choose from, or provide a rating scale. You also have to decide how the poll should behave.

- Where should the poll appear?Most people recommend placing it in the bottom right corner, but you can customize this.
- When should the poll appear?
- What's the trigger?
- What do we ask the visitors?

The trigger

A poll can appear for a number of reasons. In its simplest form, it will appear after a certain amount of time. Often, the goal of a homepage is to give the users different directions to go in, so it functions like a transit area. The goal isn't to keep the visitors on the homepage; the goal is to push them forward. In this case, if we see that users are spending too much time on the homepage, we can create a poll that appears 30 to 35 seconds after the visitor lands on the page.

Then, we can ask them what information they're looking for or what's keeping them from moving forward.

You can also make a poll appear on a certain page. For example, you can create a poll for the FAQ page to understand why users are going there and find out what information they're missing. Another example is to ask for feedback on your thank you page.

Segment

Segment your visitors based on their type and traffic source. You can address different user types, such as visitors, first-time users, and returning customers. Segmenting based on traffic source is also crucial. For example, you see that the visitors coming from Facebook don't convert well. Create a poll that only targets finding out what they don't like, what they're missing, or what's holding them back from becoming a customer.

Events

Lastly, you can trigger the polls based on events. This is a bit trickier, but it's definitely worth the time. In this case, you're not triggering the polls based on pages, you're triggering polls based on actions the user has to take (e.g., showing a poll when somebody subscribes or starts using a feature).

When to use polls

As a rule of thumb, apply polls when you're thinking, *Gosh, it would be great to know what they think about this page.* Visual analytics will give you insight into the behavior of the users, but polls can help you discover what they're thinking.

Good examples of when to use a poll are

- when you run into a page where users are spending too much time but don't convert. Find out why! In a poll, ask them what they're missing? They might be suspicious or don't trust something about it. Ask them why.
- Or, you can use polls to optimize your pricing pages. Ask the users about your pricing model. Ask them about how much information they need, what they're missing, and what's holding them back from signing up.
- As a final example, you can use polls to collect basic information like, "Where did you hear about us?"

Tools of the trade

Hotjar:

We already mentioned Hotjar in the section about visual analytics. You can also use their package to create polls. It's also worthwhile to follow their blogs, since they publish great articles on how to use visual analytics, surveys, and polls.

Qualaroo:

Qualaroo specializes in polls and surveys. You can create more advanced, complex polls with multiple steps and paths (e.g., what the next question will be if the user answers x).

Customer Support Tickets

People often forget about customer support, but in reality, it's a valuable tool for collecting feedback. This is pretty much what it's there for. In many companies, customer support people are the most UX minded, since they talk with the customers every day and try to solve their problems. This makes customer support a very valuable source of information. You just have to think about how to use it.

Invite your customer support representatives to a workshop! If you have a dedicated person (or several) for managing customer support, invite them to the workshop. They talk to your customers day in and day out, so they have lots of relevant information about the users' problems and needs.

Another way to utilize customer support is to analyze support tickets and emails. By looking at the support tickets, you can understand recurring problems that your users face. You can use customer support tickets and emails to validate the problems that you think have to be solved.

Are you using an online chat? Use it for UX research! Chats open up a path to your users in real time. You can do the same with polls, but this is more interactive. Most online chat platforms offer triggering options as well—just like polls. Likewise, you can ask visitors if they're lost, if they're searching for something, or if perhaps they've run into an error. Just think of it as if you're buying shoes and the sales assistant comes over to help you.

Test type	Good for	Alternatives	Participants
User interviews	Interviews are great when you want to learn more about the target customers and validate feature ideas.	Do interviews remotely or create a UX survey.	10–15 participants
Observation	Use the observation method when you want to see how users solve the problem at the moment. It's smart to do observations on existing products to find out how users are actually using the products.	Do in-person interviews and remote interviews.	10–15 participants
Open card sort	Use open card sorts when you're curious about how people would group information with no constraints. This is a great technique to get a high-level idea for navigation.	Do it remotely.	15 participants if conducted live, 20–30 if done remotely

Test type	Good for	Alternatives	Participants
Closed sort	Use closed card sorts when you want to see how users would group information with given groups. This is especially useful to fine-tune navigation.	Do it remotely.	15 participants if conducted live, 20–30 if done remotely
Tree testing	Reverse (or tree) testing is useful when you want to find out if the information architecture is easy to understand for users.	Do it remotely.	50–60 responses per test
UX surveys	This is similar to user interviews, but on a larger scale. Use surveys to back up your interview findings with more data.	Do it remotely.	Aim for at least 100–150 responses
Polls	Use these mini "surveys" to intercept visitors and ask for bits of information right on the spot.	n/a	Aim for at least 100–150 responses, but in most cases, 30–40 responses will probably be significant

Test type	Good for	Alternatives	Participants
Analytics	Identify low-performing pages and places in the user journey where improvement is needed.	n/a	n/a
Visual analytics	Gain visual insight to how users are interacting with the website or app. This is useful for backing up usability test findings.	n/a	Depends on the type of analytics and traffic

#3 Explore

Sketch The First Ideas

In the next two chapters (Explore and Define), we're going to lay down the design foundations by moving from sketching to detailed wireframes. Sketching is not just about being low-fidelity. The focus of the Explore phase is to experiment with different approaches by looking at various solutions to a problem before we commit ourselves and flesh it out.

If you think about it, architects do the same thing. They design the floor-plan of a building before they begin adding the finer details like what kind of bricks will be used or what color the walls will be (it's not even their job to plan out these details!). When building a digital product, our foundation is the wireframe.

Wireframes are black and white outlines of a website's screens or those that will appear on an app. Wireframes represent the layout of a screen and display every element and function. Information architecture comes to life when designing wireframes because the most important decision is where to place things on the screen. What do we want the user to focus on? To maintain this focus, it's best not to use colors in your wireframes.

What are wireframes good for?

- You can design any screen easily and see how to build up the information architecture.
- Wireframes force you to deal with structural questions like, "Where should I put this element?" separately from design-related questions like, "What color should I use for the CTA?"
- You can see how the product will look very early in the process. This enables you to have discussions, iterate, and present your ideas to stakeholders from very early on.
- Wireframes let you see and test out the most important ideas and solutions.

Who can create wireframes?

It's not just the designers who can create wireframes. Much like during the planning stage, the Design phase is also a collaborative process. It's best to involve your team in the sketching phase in order to cash in on more ideas. At the end of this chapter, we're going to look at a good exercise called Design Studio to design and solve problems collaboratively.

I like to invite designers, developers, and product managers to sketch together. If we involve developers from the start, they'll be part of the process. They'll also understand the designs better, so they'll already understand the product by the time they start working on it. Also, by involving developers, you can discuss design solutions not just from the business and design standpoint but also from a technical perspective. Designers can bring in a lot of ideas, and developers know what it takes to build a product—you can find the sweet spot between the two.

Sketching

Before creating a digital wireframe, it's best to start by sketching it out on paper or a whiteboard. The point of sketching is to experiment with different ideas and sketch a screen, or a set of screens, in a fraction of the time it takes to do a digital wireframe. Use the sketches to build up screens and flesh out the flows that you designed earlier.

When you sketch, the focus is on the layout and functions. Don't worry about being accurate in size and writing detailed copy. That's why it's called low-fidelity. The goal is to feature every element that has to go into a screen. Also, remember to experiment with different solutions. For example, if you're designing the product page of an e-commerce site for mobile, you can prioritize and organize the layout in lots of different ways. It might not be your first sketch that best serves the users. Since it takes very little time and energy to come up with two or three versions of a screen, this is a good time-saving advantage.

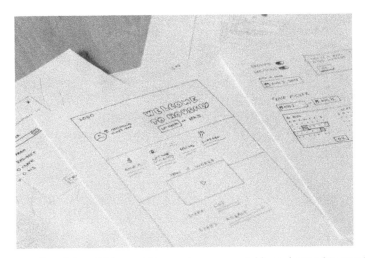

Always sketch first! This enables you to move quickly and experiment with different design solutions.

I always go as far as I can with lo-fi sketching; I design all of the screen and every possible element and interaction. Does that sound strange? Well, it's not a designer thing, nor do I love to use reams and reams paper. The real reason behind this is that it's much quicker and easier to iterate in this phase. The further along you go in the design process (creating wireframes, then pixel-perfect visual designs), the harder and more time consuming it will become to change and reframe ideas.

For example, when I designed an event organizer platform with my team that had a lot of interactions and functions (like building up the program of a conference, adding talks, inviting speakers, etc.), we kept it on paper as long as we could. Since there were complex interfaces, we had to experiment with two to three different layouts until we found the right solution, then we moved into digital wireframing. It would have been a huge waste of time to do digital wireframes, since they're harder to iterate.

Digital wireframes are not just prettier, they're also more detailed than sketches.

Digital wireframes

Once you have your sketches, you can take the next step and create digital wireframes. The focus when creating digital wireframes is the final layout, dimensions, and all the elements and copy. Wireframes represent the final structure of the screens. We have to design and prototype each function (buttons, forms, etc.). There are no colors and images, but everything is in place. A UX designer or visual designer usually creates the digital wireframes, since it's important to have interaction design knowledge and skills. However, the tools are very simple to use, so anyone can sit down and create a digital wireframe.

Wireframe prototypes

It's difficult to understand a flow or process based on static screens. Think about the checkout process of an e-commerce platform. It's easy to get lost in the information if you can't click through the screens. That's why we're going to create clickable prototypes from wireframes (so-called click-thru prototypes). "Prototype" might sound fancy, but it simply means linking a bunch of images together. The wireframe prototype is the first moment in the design process when everyone can see how the product will look and how will it work. You can present it to the stakeholders and users as well.

Prototypes come in different fidelities. The basic ones only let you walk through the product, but there are tools with which you can create full-blown prototypes that behave almost like the finished, coded product with transitions and animations.

Exercise: Four steps to design any screen

I know it's difficult to get started with sketching the design of a screen. There's the layout, functions, and content that have to go into the screen. I came up with a great technique that will ensure you won't miss anything and will keep you focused on the priorities. You won't always need to do all four steps.

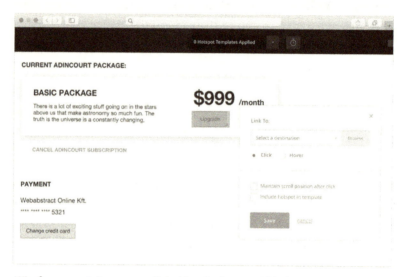

Wireframe prototypes are clickable wireframes. This lets you see how the screens are connected.

Step 1: Collect the elements

Before you can start sketching the screen, you have to know which elements (functions and content) to display on the screen. This is like a checklist for the design. You can write this checklist in a spreadsheet or simply make a list on a sheet of paper. To get started, use the materials you already have:

- The design brief

- Relevant user stories
- Task flows

Also, ask these questions:

- What elements should we show on this screen?
- What functions should we display?
- What content do I have to design (e.g., copy, images, videos, etc.)?
- From a navigational standpoint, how does this screen blend smoothly in the flow?

EXAMPLE:

You have to design a mobile app that allows you to order coffee to go. There's a screen where you have to pick the type of coffee you want. To get started, list all the possible elements that you have to place on the screen:

- Types: Cappuccino, Espresso, Latte Macchiato
- A specified image and a name for each type
- Information that explains what type of coffee options there are for those not familiar with the types
- Navigation (backward and forward in the process)

Step 2: Design the individual elements

An interface is built up of two things: elements and layout. Designing each element first is good for making sure each element is usable on its own (e.g., a button, form, or function). This is extremely useful if you have to deal with a complex interface with lots of functions to display. Designing each element ensures that you don't mess up the interface, while the layout determines where you put each element

When you design each element that has to go on a screen, you know how many elements you need to put in the layout and how they work on their own. By doing this, you can avoid a situation where something is left out; it's difficult to put another element into the design without being too complex or overwhelming.

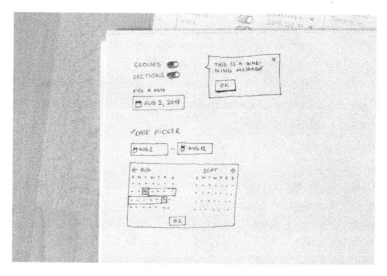

Designing the individual elements comes in handy if you're working on a complex interface, such as a web app.

In addition, the layout must not determine how an element should work. A huge number of usability issues come up because of this. For example, a designer leaves very little room for the search bar at the top right corner of the screen. This is a poor design, and you will have to rethink the structure to fit everything in. If you want the product to be useful to users, you'll need more space to add filters and shortcuts.

When you're sketching, you'll often run into elements that aren't standard, and you might not know how to design them. In this case, designing each element on its own lets you play around and experiment to find the best solution.

Step 3: Creating the layout

The layout and the elements build up the information architecture itself. When you design the information architecture and the layout, you have to decide which elements to put where. This question comes down to hierarchy and prioritization. Which elements should get more attention? What are the priorities on the screen? How will the layout help users navigate, and how will it serve the business goals?

With that said, before putting the layout and elements together, it's best to focus on the layout independently. When designing the layout, you don't care about how the elements look (we have a separate step for that). You're only focusing on the content and logical structure.

I know this might sound a bit abstract, so let me put it this way: When an artist starts to paint a picture, they first create an outline on the canvas that they can fill in later with figures, colors, and background. This outline will reflect what the artist wants the viewer to focus on and what the hierarchy is between the elements that can be seen. However, unlike painting a picture, in some cases, you can change the order and start by designing the layout and structure first, before designing the individual elements. For example, when I design a landing page or a site with lots of content, I prefer to sketch the basic blocks of content before going into detail.

Designing the layout separately is essential with complex sites. If you think about a landing page, the "what to put where" question can make or break the experience. If the users don't find it relevant and don't quickly find the information they are looking for, they leave.

When designing for mobile devices, the layout is extremely important. You don't have much space, so you have to prioritize wisely and make sure that the crucial elements are easily accessible and usable.

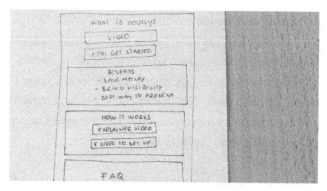

Sketching the layout without the individual elements will help you focus on the big picture. What's important? What's less important? How can you build up the information architecture?

Here are a few tips for creating a better layout:

- Sketch blocks of content (like headers, navigation, etc.)—don't design the individual elements.
- Use vertical prioritization. The higher you position an element, the more attention it gets. As a rule of thumb, the more important a function or piece of content is for the users (and for the business), the higher you should place it.
- Look up design patterns and what people are used to. It's crucial to build on information that people already know. If something works as we expect, we feel relieved that it's not taxing to use.
- Try two to three different layouts before jumping into the details. I know from professional experience that the first version is usually not the one that works best.

Step 4: Putting it all together

As a final step, bring everything together and sketch the whole screen. Start by drawing the layout, then add the detailed elements.

148

Like I said earlier, it's worthwhile to be as precise as possible; it doesn't take much time to flesh out a sketch on paper.

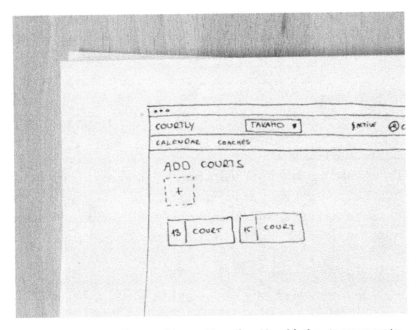

The final screen with everything put together. Now it's time to move on to the digital wireframes!

Always lead the user!

A good interface takes the user by the hand and walks them through the design. They always know where they are, what to do, and how to navigate. However, when designing a product, it can be a challenge to keep all of this straight. Therefore, you should use the questions below, and ask them for every screen. These questions will ensure that every screen is straightforward, there are no holes in the process, and the navigation is easily usable.

1. What is this screen?

The first type of question that everyone asks when opening up a page, downloading an app, or looking at an interface is, "What is this screen?" "Where am I?" "What's the purpose of this screen?" As a user, you have to identify which page you're currently on. If you don't know, you get confused. If you don't know, you leave.

Question to ask
Is it clear to the users what this screen is?

2. What can I do here?

The second thing you want to find out on a page is what you can do there. What functions can you use? For example, you want to know if this is the place to sign up, buy something, create a profile, or order a coffee. As a user, it has to be clear what the screen is about and what it is used for.

Question to ask
Is it clear to the users what the screen is for?

3. How can I move forward?

The third question is all about navigation. What's the next step? How can I get started or move forward in the process? Think about a checkout process! As a user, you have to be able to quickly understand what you need to do to move forward to the next step (e.g., fill in your information, choose a payment method, review the order, or pay). Make sure that the users can easily understand how to use the navigation.

Question to ask
Can users quickly identify how to use the navigation and move forward to the next screen?

If you can answer these three questions with a resounding "yes," that's great! However, if you feel it's not always straightforward, go back and work on it. Another good tactic is to ask others to give a fresh perspective on the designs and tell you what they think.

EXPERT ADVICE: Run five-second tests!

The best way the make sure you've got the three questions covered is to do five-second tests on them. Head over to the Validate chapter, where I show you a brilliant technique called five-second tests. Use this technique to show the wireframes or designs to the users for exactly five seconds, then do the following:

- Ask them to identify what each page is about.
- Ask them to tell you what they think they can do on the page.
- Ask them to show you how they would move forward.

For the last question, you could also apply a click test (so the users can click through the design).

Practical tips for creating better sketches

As with everything, practice makes perfect. If you follow the tips below, you will create far better sketches.

- When creating the list of elements, list them on the side of the paper or whiteboard as a checklist.
- Don't use too much space at once! On A4 paper, you can draw five to six desktop or mobile screens. This way, you'll get a better

overview of the screens and save a lot of space (and paper).

- Sketch a browser or frame for the mobile! This will help you keep the dimensions and focus on the device.
- Add labels to the screens! This might sound like a no-brainer, but a lot of people do sketches without labeling them. Later on, it's difficult to organize and identify the screens. It's especially important to do this when you draw different states (like what happens during a mouse hover). So, always write the names of the screens above them.
- Be clear! The text should be readable. Erase redundant drawings from the board. If something isn't clear and straightforward, redraw it. Never scribble! It doesn't have to perfect, but it should be readable and clean.

Go green! Sketching on a tablet

Even though we talked a lot about sketching on paper, we shouldn't neglect to mention using tablets like an iPad for lo-fidelity design work. In the past few years, I've moved completely away from using paper in my design process. Don't get me wrong; I loved working with paper—I'm a bookworm. I love the smell, texture, and feel of paper. But as a design tool, paper isn't exactly user-friendly. Just think about it.

- It's difficult to utilize all the empty space without making a mess.
- You can't rearrange or move elements.
- If you make a mistake, there's no way to efficiently erase it.
- It's difficult to stay organized.
- You need a lot of paper.

The last point was really bugging me. I try to be environmentally conscious, and I knew it wasn't environmentally friendly to use tons of paper just to throw it all away. The same goes for Post-its. They're just lovely, aren't they? It makes a UX designer's heart beat faster when they see a wall covered in Post-its. But using Post-its generates a lot of waste. So, try to use Post-its only when you absolutely have to.

Back to sketching! The newer generations of iPads with the Apple Pencil make it very easy to create lo-fidelity sketches. But I'm not here to promote Apple; I'm sure you can do just as well with other tablets and pens. Using a tablet for sketching has numerous benefits.

Digital sketching lets you iterate on your sketches

One of the most frustrating things about using paper was the inability to make changes to a sketch. If I wanted to change parts of a sketched layout, I had to redraw the whole thing. If you're using a tablet, this is no longer an issue. You can erase and redraw your sketches, copy and paste elements, and add or remove details.

Clean sketches

Digital sketching allows you to do clean work by refining the sketches and removing unnecessary scribbles from the document. Keeping the document clean enables you to share it with clients or team members; you won't be embarrassed about your sketches.

Higher speed and higher fidelity

Digital sketching creates a new fidelity that I call "high-fidelity sketching." There are lots of details in this high-fidelity sketch. The best part is the ability to add copy to the design. Using an iPad (or another tablet), you can zoom in and actually write the copy for the design right in the lo-fidelity sketch! Crazy, right? It's extremely useful. Instead of just drawing lines to represent the text, you can work in actual microcopy. I sketched icons and tweaked this interface multiple times before I was satisfied with the layout. This would have been impossible on paper. Back then, I would have probably done some sketches on paper and then sat down with my laptop to put together the layout using a design tool. Now, I prefer to experiment and tweak the layout on an iPad; it's much faster.

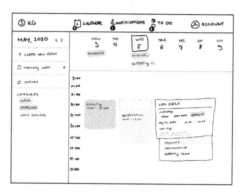

Adding icons and illustrations is a breezee

Icons and illustrations are huge in design. Using illustrations is a great way to make the product more personal and attractive. A great illustration starts with a great idea. The illustration has to be relevant and tailored to the interface—that's why you need a good idea. For example, if you want to design a 404 screen, you could create an illustration of an empty birdcage with the door open and some feathers flying out from the inside. Cool, right? And you don't need to be an illustrator to come up with this kind of idea. If you love doing illustrations, that's awesome, but if you don't, you can still sketch out a concept and have somebody create it for you. The same goes for icons. Instead of using an icon library, you can just sketch out whatever you think is most relevant in that particular case. You can use an icon library later on, when doing the digital format of the designs, but for sketches, I like the freedom of focusing on the content versus the technical execution. Digital sketching allows you create content—textual or visual—without technical barriers.

Here are some tips for sketching on an iPad:

- Don't just sketch screens; draw flowcharts, mind maps, anything that will help you think through how to solve the design problem at hand.
- Use different stroke weights to create visual hierarchy. Bold strokes are great for headings or drawing larger objects. Thin lines make it possible to zoom in and add text to the sketches.
- Add as much copy to the screens as possible! Add labels to buttons, write copy for the headings, and name all the navigation elements.
- Name the screens in your sketches. A quick but very useful tip is to name your screens so anyone can identify what that screen is about—like naming artboards and frames in design files.
- Create empty states and onboardings and add illustrations to them. I'm not a great illustrator, but I always sketch something out very early on. Later, I decide whether I can put together the high-fidelity illustration or I need to hire somebody to do it for me.
- Keep your sketches clean! Delete everything you don't need! Arrange the screens in a way that makes sense.

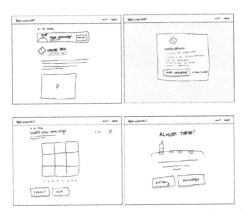

iPad sketches for a sudoku app, Brainsword. I created copy for the instructions while doing the sketches.

Exercise: The Design Studio

The Design Studio is not a place, it's an exercise—it may be the most important activity for product designers. During a Design Studio session, the team focuses on a design problem or designs a particular screen together. Anyone can request a Design Studio session. For example, if a designer is stuck with a problem, a session is a great way to get others involved and solve the problem with fresh eyes.

At the beginning of the Design Studio session, the facilitator describes the problem that the team has to solve. The facilitator makes sure everyone understands the challenge and the goals. Then, everyone works independently for 15 minutes to sketch as many solutions to the problem as they can think of. When time's up, the team discusses each solution and determines if more rounds of sketching are needed. The outcome? Lots of great, viable ideas to work with.

When should I hold a Design Studio workshop?

I like to hold a Design Studio workshop when I first launch a project so everyone on the team is involved from day one. As a general rule, it's best to begin by designing the difficult or risky interfaces, such as those that have lots of elements or content (e.g., the main page, the product page of an e-commerce site, or the most complex screen you have in your app). It's worthwhile to have multiple ideas for these screens; hosting a Design Studio workshop will help you get on the road to success.

Another great time for a Design Studio workshop is when somebody is stuck on a problem or needs new ideas and input in order to continue working. I'm sure you know the feeling of being deeply involved in something where a set of fresh eyes could be a huge help. You get a wide range of ideas during a Design Studio workshop. A product manager will provide valuable ideas because they know a lot about the product and the business goals. Inviting a developer to sketch can also be very beneficial. Developers will be more focused on the technical details and constraints, and this comes in handy when you want to solve a problem.

Don't criticize!

The point of a Design Studio exercise is to generate ideas. It's crucial that ideas that are cooking during a session are not criticized. At the end of the session, it's up to the designers to determine which ideas to implement in the design.

Make it clear to all the participants that they're there to generate ideas, not to review or criticize. This will help everyone come up with better ideas, and it will create a relaxed, thoughtful environment for brainstorming.

Don't get me wrong; everyone on the team should be encouraged to express what they like about a particular idea, as giving positive feedback during a Design Studio session works well. But it's not about building self-confidence. It's about identifying good ideas and building on other people's ideas.

Nurturing new habits

Holding a Design Studio session one time is good; doing it regularly is great. Regularity is especially important when somebody is stuck with a problem. I know from experience that it's difficult to stop the production line and run over to help somebody, but having a regular meeting time for a Design Studio workshop will provide you with a good framework. Book a meeting room for the same time each week. This way, you'll have to collaborate. Believe me, you'll always have topics to discuss!

How to host a Design Studio workshop:

Duration	Who to invite	Prepare
One hour	Product manager Designer Stakeholders	Whiteboard Pen Paper

Prepare the stage.
Book a meeting room for 120 minutes. You'll probably want paper, pens, and a whiteboard (but you can live without these things). Invite three to five people to the session.

Present the problem.
Explain the problem or discuss what screens need to be designed. If you have an existing design that you want to improve (e.g., a screen you're not satisfied with), talk about it so that everyone understands the challenge and what needs to be done. I don't like to show the designs we already have in order to ensure there is no bias during brainstorming. You want fresh ideas, not iterations. If you're designing new screens together, use the relevant user stories, storyboards, and info from the design brief.

Work individually for 15 minutes.
Have the group sketch individually for 15 minutes. This might seem like a short amount of time, but the goal is to create as many different ideas as possible in 15 minutes. If you're designing new screens, sketch as much from the flow as possible. This is a brainstorming exercise; don't limit yourself, and don't criticize your work. Just throw everything on the

table; the designers will pick the ones that work best. In a great Design Studio session, people aren't stressed about their ideas and how they'll be perceived. Just relax and sketch.

Present the ideas to the team.
When time's up, present your ideas to the team. Put the sketches on the board or wall, then go through them one by one and discuss the designs. When you present your ideas, focus on explaining why you think they could work. You can also do a round of positive voting so everyone can express what they like about the designs.

Steal and continue sketching.
The session often ends here. You have the information you were looking for, and you can continue working. However, sometimes it's a good idea to do a second round to refine the ideas and build on other people's sketches. In this second round, you have to steal from other people. Use the things that you liked about a particular solution and make a better version. This is fun and easy because, during the presentation, you will have lots of ideas on how to improve your design. During the second round, you'll have the chance to show them to the team.

Close the session.
As I mentioned, the Design Studio session is for generating great ideas. With that said, when the session is over, the designers collect the sketches and go back to work on them. They have to choose which ideas to implement and which to exclude.

Brainstorm more ideas!

An alternative version of the Design Studio exercise is to divide each paper into six equal sections. The task is for everyone to sketch six different solutions to a problem. The best time to use this technique is when you have a particular design problem to solve. A good example is the design of a mobile app's feed screen. The goal is to use the space wisely, prioritize functionality, and have the most used functions in a handy place. To get the best result, you'll have to experiment with lots of different solutions.

Key takeaways

- Always start by sketching the app or website screens before venturing into digital wireframing. Use a pen and paper or sketch on a whiteboard.
- Use the four steps we covered for designing a screen. Collect every element you should design, design the individual elements, create the layout, and put it all together.
- It's crucial that the users can identify what each screen is good for and what they can do there. Use five-second tests to make sure visitors can instantly understand the purpose of the page, what can they do with it, and how they can navigate their way through the product.
- Create a paper prototype for experimenting with different ideas. When you want to test your ideas, digitize the sketches and create a click-thru prototype from them. This way, you can show it to stakeholders and users in a fraction of the time.
- Do a Design Studio exercise with your team to design screens and solve problems in a collaborative way; this exercise is great for brainstorming and generating ideas, so do it often.

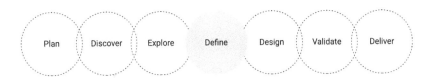

Plan | Discover | Explore | Define | Design | Validate | Deliver

#4 Define

Flesh Out The Wireframes

Once you have the sketches, you can move on and create digital wireframes. It's easy to get started in the Define phase since we've already worked things out on paper or a whiteboard in the Explore phase. After you have all the sketches, the next step is to use software to refine the designs. The goal is to finalize the structure and the copy.

When creating digital wireframes, you go into more detail than with sketches. A digital wireframe will show the final layout and dimensions of the screens. If it's a mobile design, this will be the resolution of the device. If it's for the web, you'll be working with the usual screen resolutions (1366x768, 1920x1080, etc.). Wireframes feature all the content and functionality displayed on a screen: buttons, inputs, icons, image placeholders, and copy. As we move forward, we'll discuss copy at length because it's one of the most important and overlooked things in UX.

Having said all this, the focus of the Define phase is to clarify the sketches and create detailed wireframes. The goal is to display all the elements and content and finalize the structure of each screen. In the next part of the Design phase, we'll add colors, images, and create the pixel-perfect layout, but we won't make any changes to the structure.

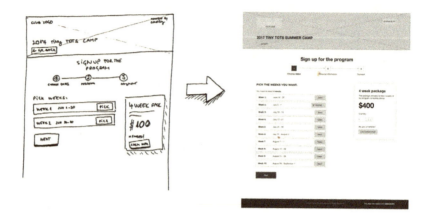

The same screen shown as a sketch and as a digital wireframe.

Can I skip sketching and start creating digital wireframes right away?

Yes, of course you can, but it's not recommended. You can sit down and start creating the digital wireframes, but I would recommend sticking to sketching first. It's so much faster to put together a bunch of screens without using software, searching for icons, and pushing pixels.

If you start digitally, it's much easier to get lost in the details. Don't get me wrong; there's a place for detailed wireframes, but first you have to get the core structure right. Also, if you spend too much time on a wireframe, it's much harder to throw it away when you find out it's not working. Throwing away a paper sketch? No problem!

So, take my advice and sketch your ideas first. Think of it as creating a draft version. You can imagine, experiment, and doodle while being unafraid of making mistakes. Then, once you have the basics down, you can start digital wireframing and clean everything up.

162

Who creates digital wireframes?

Ideally, a UX designer or visual designer creates the wireframes. You need solid knowledge in interaction design to create great wireframes. However, wireframing should be common knowledge throughout the product team.

Most of the tools used for creating digital wireframes are straightforward and easy to learn. At the end of the day, you're just adding rectangles, circles, and text—there's no magic here. Wireframing is a useful practice for product managers and stakeholders to try out because this is when you start to understand the questions and challenges of product design and understand how interaction design works.

My advice is for everyone to try to practice wireframing. Yes indeed! You can learn a lot about the users and the work of the designers from it. However, it's best if a UX designer with a strong background in interaction design leads the wireframing.

Start creating digital wireframes

Choose a wireframing tool.
You need a great tool for creating digital wireframes. There's a wide range of tools with different capabilities, and you need to choose the one that best suits your needs. We'll take a look at a few tools later in this chapter.

Collect everything you'll need for the design.
Obviously, you need the paper sketches. It's also imperative to prepare the relevant user stories, task flow diagrams and sitemaps. If you have a sitemap, it will give you a great overview of all the pages you have to design. A task flow diagram will help you keep track of every possible way that users

can interact with the product. This will ensure that there are no dead ends in the process. Lastly, open up the design brief and use a checklist so you don't forget any user needs or functions.

Start wireframing!

You can start with a blank document or use a template. Most of the wireframing tools come with built-in templates and wireframe kits to make your life easier. They feature common elements like image placeholders, tab navigation, icons, and even premade panels like calendars or payment screens. If you're just getting started with wireframing, I recommend looking into templates in order to learn a few techniques and ways to display common elements.

Once you have a background in wireframing, skip the templates and start from scratch. This will force you to focus on the product, not on hunting for shortcuts and adjusting premade panels to match the design that you're working on.

Always adjust the designs to match the device you're working with. If you're designing for desktop or the web, you should optimize for 1200px; this will look nice on the most common screen resolution (1366px). If you're designing for a mobile device, look up the resolution of the specific device (e.g., 375x667px for the iPhone 7). You don't have to remember these resolutions (every wireframing tool has the common screen sizes built in), you just have to pick the one you want to work with.

Start with the most complex interface you have (or the most important one). This can be your main page, the product page of an e-commerce site, the dashboard of a mobile app, or the most complex screen in your web application. Pick the one that has the most elements (functions, buttons, content, etc.). The benefit of starting with the most difficult screen is that you can see and solve the biggest challenges in the product right away.

When designing a particular screen, start with the bigger blocks and the frame of the screen. For example, design the header and footer for a website. Create the navigation and place the most important elements on the screen. Make sure you get the frequently appearing elements right (like CTAs). Then, continue to break down and create the detailed wireframe.

Don't use colors!

Avoid using colors on your wireframes; leave everything in grayscale. This will help you focus on the information architecture and the arrangement of the elements. We'll add the colors later, in a different phase. Create the structure first!

Use icons!

Icons play an important role in design. The human mind can process visual information a lot faster than it can process text. Therefore, a relevant icon can help users understand the interface better and more quickly. Icons also make designs look neat and easily scannable. You don't have to insert the final icons at this stage. We just want to show that there will be an icon representing x in the design. The goal is to be clear on what you want to communicate by using the icon, not to finalize the design. There are several icon libraries to help you get started. I recommend the Noun Project. There are also wireframing tools that offer thousands of built-in icons (e.g., UXPin).

If you're designing for mobile, check it on your mobile.

If I were to create a law for UX design, it would be that mobile designs must be checked on a mobile device no matter what you're designing for—a smartphone, tablet, smartwatch, or TV—the design must be checked on the device users will be using. More and more software offers a live preview of functionality that allows you to monitor the designs in real time on your phone or tablet. UXPin can send the wireframes directly to your mobile phone; Sketch has an app called Sketch Mirror that shows your design on mobile while working on it in real time. In the next chapter, we're going to discuss mobile design in detail (e.g., the usual hand positions and requirements to be considered when designing for mobile devices).

Images and placeholders

I wanted to dedicate a section solely to images because it's common practice to use image placeholders instead of images in wireframes (as seen below).

The well-known placeholder sign. Surely it can be used for anything, right?
Nope.

This is a good way to stop thinking about what the image should represent, but this placeholder doesn't tell us anything about what will be shown here. Also, placeholders can easily get out of hand in a wireframe.

One of the top design mistakes is putting loads of placeholders into the wireframe without thinking about their content. This is a problem because, when it comes to inserting the images, nobody knows what the placeholders are for.

Look at the wireframe below. What picture should be shown? Is there a need for a picture at all? Or, did the designer just think, We need to beef up the layout, so let's put an image here.

A wireframe with placeholders and dummy text. Do you know what the hell is going on here?

My number one concern with placeholders and lorem ipsum is that when creating wireframes, we're designing the information architecture. We decide which information to put where. An empty placeholder doesn't contain any information. It's like saying, "Let's place SOMETHING here." An easy way to solve this is to add labels to the placeholders.

Labeling the image placeholders

When you add an image placeholder to the wireframe, you should add a label explaining what the image should represent and why it is important (see the example below). Without labeling the placeholders, it's difficult to understand what's what on the screen. But it magically makes sense after adding the labels.

Same wireframe, but the images are labeled. Now you'll know what pictures to insert when doing the visual designs.

The problem with empty placeholders is that they affect how the team and stakeholders perceive the wireframes. This means you can't do usability tests with a wireframe that has no text (like the one above) because this would cause a lot of users to stop and think about what they're seeing (or not seeing), and this could create bias.

Use of images in wireframes

It's standard practice and a general rule of thumb to not use images in wireframes; the point of placeholders is to save time. There's no need to look for images; just create a placeholder and explain what should go there later in the Design phase. However, sometimes you have to break this rule. To put it simply, use images if it's difficult to understand the screen without them.

Take a look at the example below. The screen shows the location of a shop. It would be difficult to figure out what's going on without displaying the map. As you can see below, I've inserted the map nicely and made it gray-scale; it's easy and straightforward.

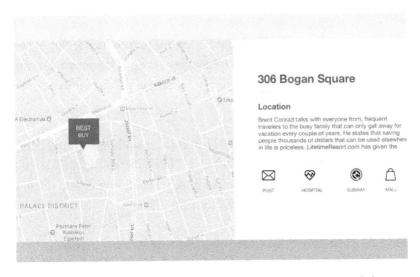

It's not a crime to use images in wireframes. Sometimes, you simply have to use them! This map wouldn't make much sense if it was just a placeholder.

Dump lorem ipsum

The other big challenge with wireframes is the copy. The copy is one of the most important elements in UX. Unfortunately, it's often overlooked. Many times, small instructional text (the so-called microcopy) has a bigger impact on the usability and overall experience than the design itself.

Every designer knows lorem ipsum. We're wired this way. But, it's bad practice to use it in UX. Originally, lorem ipsum was used by pressmen and in desktop publishing (DTP). They needed some text to fill in for content that had not yet been produced. The text itself is a scrambled section of a Latin text by Cicero from the 1st century BC. It's been altered and filled with dummy words to make it nonsensical. Okay, end of history lesson.

Lorem ipsum is good for DTP, but it's terrible for product design. Why? Because you're not just designing the appearance of the content, but the content itself. When you're designing information architecture, you can't do so with a dummy text.

A lot of designers still use lorem. They create a landing page and don't have to think about the content. It's easy. They just throw in some lorem, and they're good to go. But, just like placeholders, lorem ipsum doesn't provide any information about the content.

Here are some reasons for NOT using lorem ipsum for wireframes:

- If you use lorem, you won't think about what content you need on the screen; you just insert the placeholder. Maybe you don't need any text at all.
- It's easy to sit back and focus on the appearance of the screens and

forget about content. "A paragraph of text would look nice here." Fail. Don't let visuality dictate what information will be displayed. It should be the other way around. Think about what the users want to see, and design for that.

- The lorem will have to be replaced anyhow. Sometimes, nobody knows what the lorem was originally for, so it gets deleted even though users might have needed that information.
- When you replace lorem with the real content, things can get messy. What happens when you have to put a lot of text where you just had a few words or vice versa when there's no need for content and the design ends up empty after deleting the lorem?

In the example below, you can see the interface of a web application for organizing events. The most complex screen is the timeline where you can see the event program. You can add talks, workshops, breaks, and so on. As you can see, if we only use placeholder text (not lorem, but not real content, either) the layout looks nice. There are just a few words that are easily readable and look neat. But, when you insert the REAL content, things get messed up. Usually, the title of a presentation is longer than two words, and a speaker's name can be as many as three words. You have to be prepared for these things.

Real content can mess things up. The best way to avoid these problems is to always use real content and consider edge cases.

1. Write labeling copy!

As we discussed, when we're designing wireframes, we're designing information architecture. Labeling copy lets you know how long a particular piece of text needs to be and what the text should be about. This is not the final copy of the website or app. You should use it to replace nonsensical lorem ipsum with something that provides information for the user.

In the below image, on the left, all we can see is that there's larger text that's probably more important than the smaller text below it. On the right side, we can see that the larger text is the title of the article. Since titles are rarely two words long, we used longer text here to be as close to the real content as possible. We even have a place to hint at how to write the real content so that it's beneficial and relevant to the users. We can also see that there is a description of the article below.

EXAMPLE:

Lorem ipsum

Lorem ipsum dolor sit amet, consectetur adipiscing elit. Ut nunc massa, malesuada nec mauris ac, auctor tincidunt urna.

Engaging article title that typically contains a number as well

This is a description of the article, the so called 'lead'. It should briefly sum up the whole article to lure visitors in reading the content.

Labeling copy in action on the right.

What makes good labeling copy?

- It describes the content of the text.
- It gives you an idea of how much actual text you'll need to place there.
- It's similar to the length of the real content. For example, if you need two to three lines of lead for an article, you don't insert 600 words of text, as the page will fall apart. Replacing two to three

172

words of text with nine to ten words, like in the example above, is even more dangerous.

But I'm a designer, not a copywriter!

Dear designer friend, if you feel that it's not your job to think about copy, I have bad news for you—it is the job of a UX designer. As a UX designer, we go even further in developing copywriting skills. This is because the users will understand a number of things from the copy on the website or in an app. If they don't understand something because the copy is bad, that means the UX is bad. Everyone can write labeling copy. It's not Dickens, it's just simple and informative text. If you have difficulties writing copy, try to think of it as explaining something to a friend. Imagine that your friend asks you what kind of content should go in a certain spot, and explain it to them in a few words. If you don't write labeling copy and just stick with lorem, people will keep asking you why you placed text there. The product manager will ask, the stakeholders will ask, even the developers will ask. If you don't give hints to the copywriters about how much text you need, where it should go, and what it should be about, they'll get it wrong. If developers encounter lorem and don't know what to do with it, they'll delete it. And, obviously, you can't go live with lorem in your product.

Lastly, you can't do usability tests with lorem ipsum because users won't understand a thing. You have to come up with some copy for the usability tests anyway. All in all, it's better to handle this yourself to prevent any headaches.

2. Use real content!

What do I mean by real content? I mean relevant text from other websites or products, copy you wrote yourself, or text from your existing product.

Whenever you can, use real content. This will give everyone who looks at the wireframes an idea of how the real content will look.

More and more tools offer ways to insert real content into the design. For example, InVision's Craft is an extension for Sketch and Photoshop. With it, you can generate headlines, articles (on various topics), names, cities, and much more and insert them directly into the design so you don't have to open your browser. Even better, you can copy text from an existing website with Craft (e.g., using your existing site or competing products as a source of information). Aside from text, Craft also lets you insert images without having to browse Unsplash or Pexels. Just pick a topic, and a royalty-free image is inserted.

Whenever you can, DUMP lorem when designing the screen. It might be handy sometimes, but only if you do it with labeling copy, such as when you need multiple paragraphs of text. In this case, make sure you apply labeling copy in the beginning of the paragraph to explain what content should go there, then fill the rest with lorem.

InVision's Craft allows you to generate different types of text like names, headlines, and articles. It also allows you to define the text you'll use in the designs.

The secret sauce: Microcopy

Microcopy is the secret weapon of UX. It's secret because, unfortunately, this is the most overlooked aspect in product design. Microcopy can make or break your product experience. So, what are microcopies?

- Labels and placeholders of input fields
- Success and error messages
- Instructional text helping you to perform a task or to navigate
- Navigational texts (e.g., menu names) or links
- Button text
- Text in the progress bar on an e-commerce site

Most designers don't pay attention to these peanuts. They just type something in for the button text and fill the instructional text with lorem. Marketers and copywriters tend to ignore these because they're focused on the copy that receives the most attention. They may not even be aware that these texts exist (e.g., if the designer created separate designs displaying success and error messages).

At the end of the day, it's often the developers who have to write the microcopy. You need to have text for when the user makes a mistake like typing in the wrong password or having insufficient funds on their credit card. Obviously, this is a pain in the ass for developers, and it's not their role to think about these types of text.

Microcopy is different from other text in a product because it doesn't "sell you" anything; it helps you understand a screen and perform a task. If the microcopy is bad and poorly written, it will seriously affect the overall UX and can directly affect the conversions as well. Therefore, pay attention to these little guys.

Who has to write the microcopy?

It has to be the UX designer who writes the microcopy. Their job is to make sure the product is usable, and microcopy plays a crucial role in usability. As a UX designer, you have to understand as well as represent the needs of the users. You have to help the users understand the product quickly. This includes how to navigate and perform certain tasks. Also, it's crucial to think about what happens if the users make a mistake. How can you get them back on track again?

Why is microcopy so important?

- It provides users with information on how to do something (how to fill in an input field, how to choose a payment method, or what to do if they've made a mistake).
- Badly placed or poorly written microcopy will confuse visitors. This can easily result in making the users leave the website or abandon the product.
- Microcopy has a huge impact on the overall UX. Simply improving microcopy can lead to an increase in conversions.
- Microcopy builds trust and credibility between you and your users.

For example, Veeam noticed that a lot of visitors were asking for a price. They had a "Request a quote" option on their site. They decided to test what would happen if they changed the phrase from "Request a quote" to "Request pricing." They saw an increase in clicks on their lead generation form of 161.66%. What happened here? Visitors wanted to find out the price of the product. "Request a quote" might have sounded intimidating to them. They might have thought that requesting a quote would be too time consuming, or they might have had the word "pricing" in their minds and not "quote." Either way, understanding the language of the users and writing a clean but straightforward microcopy can skyrocket the user experience.

When to write the microcopy

The best and easiest thing to do is to write the copy while doing the wireframes; it's beneficial to test the wireframes and the copy at this time. You can show it to any stakeholder or team member and collect feedback on the copy. You'll have time to work on the copy later when doing the visual designs, but it's best to start during the wireframing stage.

Follow this list to write awesome microcopies:

- Always write microcopy when doing digital wireframes.
- Write it supposing that no one will review or change it before going live. It has to be clear as well as engaging from both the UX and grammatical standpoint.
- If you're unsure about it, ask others on your team to express their opinion, or try brainstorming.
- Monitor and learn from competitors. Sometimes, this will show you how NOT to explain something.
- Microcopy is pure UX; it's about being useful over being pretty. Be as clear and straightforward as possible. Only say what you truly need to say. Believe me, the users will be thankful for this!
- Always have a dedicated time to work on microcopy!
- Double check if the copy is well placed and well written. It's easy to lose track of it, so always keep an eye out!
- Be simple and friendly. Remember that you're helping people; don't talk like a droid!
- Pay extra attention to what happens when the user makes a

mistake. A great error message can help people get back on track and convert them. A personalized success message will drive engagement and build a stronger connection between you and your users.

Positioning matters.

The wording is just one side of microcopy. Positioning is just as important. If the users don't see it, then it doesn't matter how good your copy is. A classic example of this is not displaying error messages where the error actually occurred.

Below, on the left, is an example of poor placement. I entered an invalid email address, and the error message is displayed in the bottom left-hand corner. At first, I didn't even notice it. I just kept staring intently at the middle of the screen. This makes it difficult to discover the problem and solve it. On the right, you can see a good example. "This is not a valid email address." is displayed right below the email field. The field even turns red, indicating that there's a problem. I can spot this instantly.

Bad positioning on the left, and good positioning on the right. You should always display the error message where users encounter the problem.

Make sure the positioning of the microcopy is good. To get this right, create user stories for the microcopies. Every success or error message is a story. You need to identify when and why it happened as well as how to solve it.

Test out your microcopy.

Learn from the Veeam example. Do A/B tests to test just the microcopy. Create different versions with more text or less text or a more personal or more corporate style. Remember that microcopy alone can improve your conversions. So, if you have an e-commerce site with a complex checkout, start working on the microcopy first. Focus on labels, button text, input field placeholders, and instructional text.

You can also fine tune the microcopy by doing usability tests. Pay extra attention to the copy during a usability test; it only takes seconds to change and improve it. Watch for people getting confused during the test. Is it because of misleading microcopy? What words would they use instead? You have to understand their jargon and not force them to learn the product's jargon.

Design Patterns

If I asked you where to find the login on a website, you would probably say, "It's on the top right corner." If I asked you where the logo is, you'd say, "It's on the top left corner of the page." These are conventions that we come across every day on millions of websites. A convention can cut down the learning path and save us time.

If something works the way we expect, based on past experiences, it makes us happy and thankful because deep down human beings are lazy.

Most design problems have already been given a lot of thought. Obviously, when designing a product, we don't want to reinvent the wheel. If there's a great preexisting solution, it's worth building upon. You simply save time for yourself as well as the users.

Be careful with design patterns!

Design patterns are great. They speed up the learning process and reduce the cognitive load of users. However, you should be careful with them.

- Only use design patterns that your users are familiar with (Granny, do the swipe thing!).
- Even if a lot of other products are using a specific design pattern, it can still be bad or inconvenient.

The first point is very important, and lots of people make a mistake here. Most designers love Apple stuff. They have their iPhones, Macs, and all the gadgets. I'm not having a go at them, I have all of it too. iOS has a lot of great design patterns. Moreover, there are a lot of standards for OS X on how to build up a software interface, so the users don't have to learn them from the ground up.

If you design for Android, however, you have to adapt to another environment. The patterns that users know are different. The navigation, icons, and common elements look different. It often happens that what is a well-known pattern on one device or platform is unknown on another. In the example below, you can see two patterns for sharing content. In the left image, an iOS user will automatically know that the icon in the left corner is for sharing content and transferring it to another device (e.g., with AirDrop). It's used in every Apple device; phones, tablets, wearables, laptops, and desktop computers. But it wouldn't be great to use it in an Android design, since Android has a different standard icon for sharing.

Then there's the granny example. This example draws the attention to the fact that not everybody knows the same design patterns. This can vary based on age, location, culture, prior knowledge, and many other factors. That's why when you decide to use a design pattern, you have to make sure that the target users know that pattern.

The share icon is different on iOS and Android. What might seem normal for iOS, might seem crazy for Android.

Don't fall for design patterns just because you see them used in a lot of products. That doesn't mean that they're good or convenient. If a multi-billion dollar internet company starts to use something, it doesn't guarantee that it will work for you.

One of my favorite examples of this is the hamburger menu. You know, that little icon showing three horizontal lines. This was invented by designers to hide a lot of information and navigation without destroying the layout (or having to rethink the design). Millions of sites and products use the hamburger menu, but in reality, it's like a door saying "ANYTHING." It doesn't give any information to the users about what they'll find once they click on it. People are getting used to it, but it's still a bad practice.

Another example is putting the back navigation on a mobile device in the top left corner. This is something that Apple is messing up. Is there anybody with a device larger than 4.5 inches who can tap on it without dropping their device? Again, millions of products use this pattern even though it's bad and causes problems.

All in all, look for design patterns and use them, but always think from the users' perspective. Do they know that pattern? Is it convenient? Does it speed up the learning process? Don't follow a practice just because others (especially huge companies) are using it. It might take them more time to find out that it's a bad practice. For example, nobody will abandon Apple just because the navigation is inconvenient. Make sure your design is usable by doing usability tests that allow you to test out the design patterns as well.

Where to look for design patterns

Look through the websites and apps your target users use on a daily basis.
What websites are they visiting frequently? What apps do they download? Which social media platforms are they hanging out on? These are all places you can find a pattern to use. For example, if you know your

target regularly uses Instagram, you can be sure they know how to use it and can learn from it.

Check on the competitors' products.
Be extremely careful with this one! Just because they are already in the market, that doesn't mean they know better than you. Sometimes, you'll even learn what not to do.

Visit design pattern sites.
There are some sites gathering good design patterns. They're categorized as input fields, sign-ups, navigation, empty states, and so on. This a good start, and you can get inspired by these ideas.

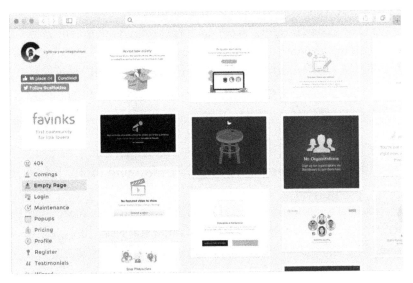

Calltoidea.com collected lots of great designs and categorized them. You can search for lots of different things (e.g., empty states or log-in screens).

Tools for creating digital wireframes

Before we dive in and see what tools are out there for wireframing, we need to clarify what prototyping is. When it comes to UX, prototyping is taking designs and making them interactive. The word prototyping is mostly used for solutions that are not created using the final technology. They are rapidly modeled to test out the ideas we have. That's why it starts with "proto," which means "first," "source," or "parent."

When it comes to wireframing tools, we can divide them into three categories:

- Tools in the first category are only good for wireframing; the outcome is an image and not a clickable prototype.
- The second category is only good for prototyping; you need to create the wireframes with another tool.
- In the third category, there are tools that are great for creating wireframes (sometimes even visual design) and prototyping at the same time.

What to look for when choosing a wireframing tool

For starters, is it only for creating wireframes, or can you do prototyping with it as well? It's not be a deal breaker, but if you pick a tool that's only good for wireframing, you'll need another one for prototyping.

Another important aspect is whether the tool has a built-in library of pre-made elements. Even if you aren't going to use the final icons in a wireframe, it's still important to have them. If the tool has a great library of elements, it will save you a lot of time. For example, there are a lot of wireframe templates and icon sets for Sketch. Figma also offers a wide range of plugins and ready-to-use icon libraries and templates.

Is it a cloud-based or desktop app? Going with the cloud means it's easier to share the wireframes, and you don't have to worry about platforms or operating systems. The drawback is that it's usually a lot slower and not as stable as desktop software. This is a concern for professional usage. Believe me, you don't want to sit in front of your computer waiting for your project to load. This is something that will improve soon though, since cloud apps are getting better and better. On the other hand, a desktop platform can also be a limitation because most apps run on MacOS.

Lastly, it's worth considering software you already know. For example, if you're a designer who uses Sketch, Photoshop, or even Illustrator, it might be good to stick with the tool you know.

Best overall wireframing and product design tool: Figma

In the earlier editions of this book, I reviewed a couple of different tools you can use for wireframing. Since then, Figma has emerged and become immensely popular. It easily checks all the boxes. Lucky for me, I'm going to only suggest one tool for you to use. I can do that because I'm 100% sure it will do the job for you and won't leave you unsatisfied. Sounds cool, right? Before we discuss what Figma can bring to the table, I have some requirements. This is what I want from a professional design tool in 2020:

- The ability to easily create wireframes and high-fidelity designs (no need to use multiple platforms)
- The ability to create click-through prototypes (more on this topic in the next section)

- The ability to easily build and maintain a design system (more on design systems in the Design chapter)
- Cross-platform usage (Mac, Windows, etc.)
- Real-time collaboration with clients and team members

Figma is a web-based design tool that ticks all the boxes above. It's very easy to learn, but it's also scalable for more serious product design work—it's different for a sole designer to work on a product versus a team maintaining an extensive design system where the collaboration is also key. Figma covers all these bases.

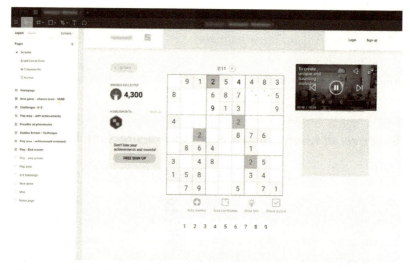

Figma is a light-weight design tool that empowers collaboration and assists in building smart design systems.

Figma for wireframing

It's very easy to get started. You can draw shapes, pull in icons, and add text just as you would with any other design software. You can also easily add plugins to Figma, which add shortcuts to make your life easier. For example, you can add icon library plugins that will allow you to search for icons inside Figma and use them in your wireframes. There's no need to step outside the system.

Figma comes with a built-in prototyping mode that's very simple to use, but is pretty effective. You just take the wireframes you've designed and link them together (similar to InVision or Marvel), then launch the presentation mode, and there you go—your wireframes are now clickable. One big advantage of this method is that you don't need to worry about updating the designs when doing the prototypes. It's all there, so whatever you see is always the latest version.

The files created with Figma are stored in the cloud. This means you can instantly share your work with your clients or send it to stakeholders or potential users. Figma designs can be opened in your browser, so the receiving party doesn't need to install any software. Since the files are in the cloud, you can invite other people to collaborate with you on the designs. You can grant them viewing access or invite them as editors. Imagine you're creating a wireframe for a website and you're working with copywriters. Without the real-time collaboration, you would need to send them the files as images or copy the content from the designs into a word doc and send it to them. Not with Figma. You can just share the designs with the copywriters, grant them editing access, and there you go—they can update the text directly in the design files.

Lastly, I have to mention that Figma is free for personal use. If you're a team and want to utilize the more advanced features Figma has to offer, you'll need to sign up for the premium plan. But for starters, the free account can go a long way. Basically, you only need to upgrade to premium when you have a team of designers and/or a more mature product with a well-established design system.

Back to prototyping

Now you understand the basics of prototyping and know about a few tools that can get you started. The main idea is to take the designs and create something interactive so you can click through them. You can prototype anything. It can be a website or a mobile app. It can be very simple or pretty advanced. The whole idea of prototyping is to save time by testing out your ideas before investing time and money in development. This way you can learn faster and eliminate unnecessary features and usability issues that could otherwise cost you money in the future.

From the UX perspective, we can divide prototypes into three categories:

- Click-through prototypes
- High-fidelity prototypes
- Coded prototypes

The click-through prototype is the most popular. The idea behind the click-through prototype is taking the designs as images, creating hotspots, and linking them together so that you can click through them. There are no animations; there are just a few basic transitions and a limited way to show interactions. It's super easy to create, no special skills are needed (like coding or months of training), and it's done in a few minutes.

The high-fidelity prototype is a big step up from the click-through prototype, with more detail and more sophisticated interactions. A high-fidelity prototype is usually based on the final visual designs and not on the wireframes. You can make the product look like the finished, real-life version with animations, transitions, and complex interactions. There are simple tools that act as design software, and there are advanced ones that require coding skills. The usual limitation of these prototypes is that you can't show dozens of pages like in a click-through prototype (otherwise it would get too complicated).

The process of creating a hotspot.

Finally, we have the coded prototypes. HTML, JavaScript, or any other programming language you prefer. Sometimes you need a coded prototype to model complex interactions.

Let me give you an example. I was working on a timeline view where you could add new events, breaks, split the timeline into two or three sections, and add events in parallel to each other. It's a challenge to design an interface like this because there are dozens of use cases and the user can go in several directions or even combine them. Now, this is something that's hard to prototype even with high-fidelity tools. I could play around with some click-through prototypes but that would always limit the users and force them to go in a certain direction. Needless to say, I wanted to find out if they could understand how the interface works, then let them do whatever they want with it. I decided to go with a coded prototype based on the wireframes, and this is how I collected feedback. I was able to learn a lot, and this would not have been possible using the other prototyping methods.

We're going to look at two prototypes: the wireframe and the design prototype. Both are click-through prototypes. The wireframe prototype is created from the wireframes. The goal with this prototype is to get feedback on the structure and copy before moving forward to implement the visual design. Design prototypes are based on the visual design and are good for testing the final layout of the product. We're going to discuss design prototypes in the next chapter.

Why create prototypes? There are two simple reasons:

- So the team and stakeholders can see what we're building
- So we can test them out with our users

Prototypes will show the team and the stakeholders how the product will look and how to use it. You don't have to show images and explain how the users will click through them. Instead, you just show them how it works.

The biggest benefit with prototypes is that they allow you to show the designs to your users and let them take them for a spin. This is what makes prototyping an essential tool for product design.

Creating wireframe prototypes

The first prototype we create during the design is the wireframe prototype. Prototyping the wireframes enables us to test out the designs at a very early stage. Since wireframes show all the elements and layout, everyone on the team can see and try out the product.

Likewise, we do wireframe prototypes so we can show them to the target users and usability test them. This provides valuable feedback and can resolve many usability issues that would otherwise surface later on in the project. Wireframe prototypes only take a few hours (if not less than one) to create, so you can test what you're building right after starting the design. Isn't that awesome? Learning and correcting errors at this stage is far cheaper than in later stages.

What are the tools for prototyping?

If you've chosen to use a wireframing tool that's also great for prototyping, this is easy. Pick UXPin, Axure, or Justinmind. However, if you've decided to stick with a design tool like Sketch or Photoshop, you'll need a prototyping tool that will make the designs clickable. A couple of great tools for this are InVision and Marvel (both work in a similar way).

Pick the tool that best suits your needs! There are more advanced tools and pretty basic ones, but they all come down to the same logic. You upload images of the wireframes or the visual designs, create hotspots, and specify which image to show when the users click on the hotspot. At the end of the Design chapter, you'll find a summary table of the top prototyping tools available on the market.

InVision

I recommend using InVision for wireframe and design prototypes. It's straightforward and has all the necessary features. You can create prototypes for the web and also for mobile that can then be displayed on your mobile device. InVision is also great for team collaboration. You can easily share the designs, and team members and clients can comment directly on the designs so you can keep track of their feedback. There's even a live share option that allows you to browse the designs together and use a virtual whiteboard, which comes in handy when you can't get together with the team or client.

In addition, InVision has a plugin called Craft, which I've mentioned a few times in this book. This plugin lets you use real data in the designs, create design libraries, and upload designs directly from Sketch or Photoshop. It also lets you create hotspots in Sketch and sync them with the cloud.

Here are some tips for making better wireframe prototypes:

- Try to think of every possible interaction, and create hotspots for everything. The more sophisticated the prototype is, the more natural it will feel to use.
- Allocate a separate time for prototyping. Creating hotspots and linking screens together is boring, but it requires precision. So, when you're getting ready to present your prototype, you shouldn't leave it to the last minute. It's better to do the prototyping in smaller chunks (not hundreds of pages at once); otherwise, it will get time consuming. Start fresh and take up the task!
- Try to look at the designs as if you are seeing them for the first time. Explore and check out every element. "What does this button do?" "How do I move forward in this process?" "Where should this link take me?" "What do users click on during the test?"
- Give yourself time to review the prototypes once you've finished them. Go through the user stories and storyboards to make sure every user need and use case is taken care of.
- If you created the prototype for a mobile device, you need to check it out on that device. Sometimes it works on the desktop, but something goes wrong on the mobile version. You don't want that to happen during a test or presentation!

192

Go for a usability test with the wireframes.

We'll go into more detail about usability tests in the Validate chapter, where we'll take a look at how to do a test step by step. For now, all you have to know is that during a usability test, you sit down with five potential users and ask them to perform a few tasks inside the product. Then, you watch them do so and take notes. The goal of the test is to find out if they could use the product with ease and find out how you can resolve any usability issues they experienced. Based on this feedback, you can make changes to the product and test it again.

Testing the wireframes is a crucial part of the process. Click-through prototypes allow us to show not just dummy pictures but a product that users can try out and click through. Most of the time, it's difficult to tell whether it's easy to use and convenient based on an image. The issues surface when you can actually use the product.

The wireframe usability test will show you if people understand the basics of your product. There are no colors, refined typography, or images, but the users still have to perform every task. Think about a payment page. Got it? Great! Now remove the colors and images, make it black and white. Done? Can you use it like this? Of course you can. Everything we removed was visual. The visuals create a feeling and can help us better understand the interface (e.g., by using color coding), but the core product can be used with just wireframes.

Take a look at the example below. On the left side, you can see the wireframe for the screen. On the right side, you can see the final visual design. There's no change in the layout; all the elements are in place, and the copy is the same. All in all, they pretty much look the same (but with/without the visual skin). This is why users have to be able to understand and use the product in the wireframing stage as well; you can test the layout, the copy, and the microcopy.

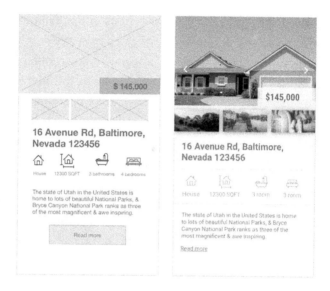

The wireframe is on the left, and the visual design is on the right.

These are some questions that can be answered by testing wireframes:

- Is the layout clear to the users? Do they understand where to find what?
- Can they complete the tasks and the process inside the product (e.g., place an order or create an event)?
- Is it easy to click-through every screen? Where does the product need to be improved? Where do the users feel lost or uncertain?
- Is the copy clear and informative? Are the microcopies well-placed and well-worded?

After you have the wireframes tested, you can go into the detailed visual designs. There will be colors, refined layout, typography, and images. Every element gets its final pixel-perfect design. Testing in the wireframe stage will show you the structural problems before adding the visuals.

Likewise, you can separate the design issues from the structural issues. For example, a button can be confusing for the users for many reasons. Is it because it uses a misleading color or because of bad placement or confusing text? If you do a wireframe test, you'll learn about the placement as well as the labeling. If the users can understand it and use it like this, but they get confused when testing the visual design, you know that something went wrong when adding the colors to the final layout (maybe the other elements received too much attention).

This is an example of bad color coding.

Let's look at a far-fetched example (above). On the left side, you can see a wireframe. On the right side, you can see a visual design. If you switch the toggle to "ON," the input field will become active so that you can fill it in and hit the "ADD" button. It's pretty straightforward. It's likely that most users will understand this quickly.

In the visual design on the right, the structure is the same, but the colors are confusing. The toggle switch is green even though it's to the left. This is strange because when the button is to the left, it usually means the toggle is "OFF" (thanks to iOS). But, it's green here. So, how does it work? Also, the "ADD" button is blue, which would typically indicate that it's active. But the toggle is "OFF," so users might think that there's no connection between the two, or they might get confused. See what I did? I only added two colors, but I made a pretty big mess. That's why it's crucial to test out the wireframes and the visual design separately.

What happens after the test?

When you're done testing the wireframes, it's time to implement what you've learned. You'll have a couple of issues to resolve. Now is the time to go back and create a better version based on the feedback. Sometimes, it's necessary to test again. The goal is to eliminate all the serious and annoying issues that come up during a test before going into the visual design.

Exercise: The Design Review

Giving feedback on the designs is important. The designers have to know what's good and where there's room for improvement. The Design Review is an exercise for the team to provide meaningful feedback to the designers.

To be honest, I don't like the word "critique." When I ask people to critique something, I'm sure they'll only focus on the negative side and only look for problems. Don't get me wrong; it's important to learn what's bad or risky about a design, but there's more to feedback than that. Everyone on a product team has to learn how to give critical but meaningful feedback to the other members (e.g., if there's a dead end in the process, or if there's a missing element on a page). We also have to pay attention to risky solutions; when users aren't aware of a technical solution, that's a potential risk (e.g., the elderly generation and gestures).

At the same time, we need positive feedback. What works well in the designs? Why is that particular solution or design good? How could we further improve a screen? Sometimes it's the positive feedback that will show you how to improve other parts of the product. If you find a great solution, you might be able to use it in other areas as well.

To give valuable and practical feedback to the designers, we need an exercise—the Design Review. During the review, the team sits down and looks at the designs. To make sure that every standpoint is covered, we'll give everyone certain roles. People with different roles will observe the designs from different perspectives. There will be roles focusing on the problems and risks and other roles paying attention to the good things. During the exercise, the team will generate a lot of ideas and feedback. Then, they'll have to decide what to implement and what to discard.

I HAVE AN IDEA!

JUST THE FACTS!

LOOK AT THE BRIGHT SIDE!

WE HAVE A PROBLEM!

Different hats, different mindsets.

We have four different roles. Each of the roles is represented by a color.

- White looks at the facts.
- Black looks for problems and potential risks.
- Yellow looks at what's good in the designs.
- Green looks for ways to improve the product.

The White Hat: "The facts, Dr. Watson, just the facts!"

If you're the white hat, your role is to look at facts and give objective feedback. Take a look at the designs and ask the following questions:

- What can we see on this screen? What can I do here? What's clear? What isn't clear?
- Do the designs fulfill every user need? Look at the design brief, the personas, and the user stories to help you figure this out. Do the designs support the business goals?
- Are the designs consistent? Are we using elements consistently across designs?
- Where do we need more input on the designs (from users, stakeholders, or clients)?
- Is the content clear and straightforward? Are the microcopies well-written and well-placed?

It's best to put the white hat in charge of the technical points as well. For example, the white hat should make sure the designs only use web fonts (for a web project) and that the designs look great on any device (desktop and mobile).

The Black Hat: "Houston, we have a problem!"

Then there's the black hat, which, of course, will focus on the dark side. The black hat gives some of the most important feedback—the critical feedback. It's no wonder everybody focuses on this one. Critical feedback is crucial to improving the designs. But first, we have to learn how to give meaningful critical feedback. If you're the black hat, consider the designs in the following way:

- What's not going to work? (e.g., "Users won't understand this screen because...")
- What are the potential risks? (e.g., "This element is great on desktop, but it doesn't work on mobile because...")
- What are the disadvantages of a particular design?

It's even more important for the black hat to back up their feedback with arguments. Maybe the most important skill to have in product design is learning how to give good arguments and feedback. We can't expect that others will always understand what the problem is with a design. I know arguing is difficult—especially for most designers. They hate defending their designs ("Why can't you see that this works?"). Designers also have to give reasons for why they think the design is great. This helps get the team on the same page. It's all about communication.

This holds true for stakeholders and leaders as well. Saying "It's not good," "It looks awful," or "I don't like it" without a viable argument is not feedback. This will result in making the designers/team unhappy and will lead to a dead end in communication. As a leader, you always have to explain why you think a particular design or solution is not viable or why you think a design looks bad. Put all of this in the context of the users; at the end of the day, we're not building products for stakeholders—we're building products for the users.

There might be a great overlap between the black and white hats. Often, they make similar remarks (mostly about what's missing), but there's nothing wrong with that. It's always great to have another set of eyes!

The Yellow Hat: "Always look on the bright side of life!"

It might sound awkward, but you can learn a lot from what's good in the designs. The yellow hat is in charge of explaining what's good about the designs and why.

- If you identify a great design solution, you can reuse it later.
- If you know what's good in the designs, you can communicate it to the others. This will be a huge help when presenting to stakeholders, clients, and investors.
- You'll make the designers and team happy by acknowledging their work. When asked to critique, people don't tend to give constructive feedback. They usually just give negative feedback, but we all like to be acknowledged. We all like to know that our work is great.

If you're the yellow hat, do the following:

- Identify what's good about the designs. Give an explanation as to why it is good and why it works.
- Identify the advantages of a particular design solution.

The "why" is crucial here. You have to know why a design is good (e.g., "This blue is great here because...") or why users will love a particular feature. The yellow hat also helps strengthen communication, which is a cornerstone of teamwork.

This is especially great training for designers (since most of them have a difficult time interpreting the designs they created). Practicing the role of a yellow hat will help you become a better communicator, which will result in less conflict and frustration.

The Green Hat: "I've got an idea!"

One of my favorite roles is the green hat. If you're the green hat, you have to think about how to skyrocket the user experience of the product or design. This is where innovation happens. The green hat has to be fresh and generate new ideas. A green hat asks questions like the following:

- What new features could we add to make the product better?
- How could we improve the designs?

Now I know this sounds intimidating. Whoa, expanding the project scope? Relax, it's not about that. But to start, every idea is welcome—even the crazy ones and the big ones that would change the project scope. Afterward, the team has to decide which ideas to implement. A green hat can come up with lots of different ideas. There might be some that are smaller and easier to implement, but they add value to the designs and improve the experience. Great new feature ideas are usually not something to implement right away, but giving space for great ideas to come to fruition is always good.

Do your first Design Review exercise!

Duration	Who to invite	Prepare
1–2 hours	Product manager Designer Stakeholders	Wireframes or visual designs Design Review template

Invite team members!

Book a meeting room for 90 minutes. Invite stakeholders, designers, researchers, and engineers to the session. Limit the number to four to six people. It's best to invite people who aren't current on the project so they can look at the designs with fresh eyes.

Set the roles.

It's best to set the roles randomly. You can learn a lot from switching roles each time. If you have more than four people in the session, start duplicating the roles (begin with the black and white hats).

Present the designs.

It's time for everyone to look at the designs. If you created prototypes earlier, they'll come in handy now. The reason I prefer to use prototypes for review (compared to printed out designs or still images) is that the team can preview the designs on the actual device. If it's a mobile app, they can preview it on their phones. So, go with a prototyping tool like InVision.

When everyone has the designs in front of them, give your presentation. The goal is to make everyone understand what screens to review. Describe the goals of the project and the product itself. Don't explain what each screen is good for (let them figure this out). Just provide the necessary information to get them started.

Work individually for 25 minutes.

It's time for everyone to start looking at the designs individually and come up with remarks based on their roles. It's worthwhile to limit this to around 20 to 25 minutes. If you need much more time than that, it's possible you're trying to review too many designs at once. If you have a lot of screens to review, break it down into chunks. You might even want to do the reviews more frequently.

In the *7STEPUX® Resource Center*, you'll find a Google Drive spreadsheet for the Design Review. In this spreadsheet, there are four tabs for each of the colors. Team members should simply open the spreadsheet and select the color (tab) they're working on. This enables the team to collect comments and remarks separately, but in one document. For each of the comments, you have to specify the location (which screen the comment is for) and the comment itself.

Discuss and prioritize!

When time's up, go through each of the comments and discuss them. Remember to back up your comments with arguments. Start with the white hat, and follow with the black hat. This will allow you to make sure that you have enough time for the most important feedback.

The team has to decide the priority for each comment and whether they'll implement it or discard it. To do this, there are two additional columns in the spreadsheet (Priority and Verdict). Since you'll end up with a lot of comments, you should prioritize ruthlessly! When you see something practical and important, make it a to-do right away.

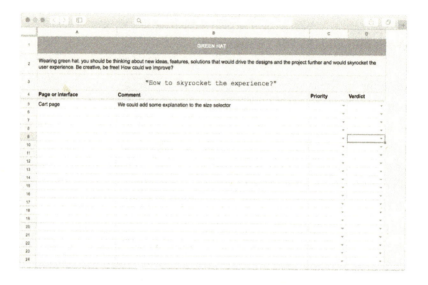

You can easily collect feedback with a simple spreadsheet.

When thinking about priority, take a look at how much time it would take to implement the comment and how big the impact would be on the user experience. The bigger the impact is—and the less time it takes to implement it—the more priority it should get.

Key takeaways

- Wireframes are fundamental to designing screens. They represent the core structure of the screens with the final layout, copy, and all the elements necessary.
- Don't use lorem ipsum in your designs. Always use meaningful text! Write labeling copy or use real content!
- Pay extra attention to microcopy. They're the bits of information that help users use the product. Microcopy can make or break the product experience, but it takes no time to sort out.
- Design patterns are conventions that are used across millions of sites and products. It's wise to follow the patterns, but always make sure the patterns are great and easy to use and that the target users know them.
- Prototyping means that we add interactions to the designs. This lets us see and test how the designs work before going into development. Creating prototypes from the wireframes enables us to see the whole product before adding visuals.
- Doing a usability test with wireframes is essential in the design process. It will show the weaknesses of the designs, and you'll be able to resolve any issues in much less time. This allows you to direct efforts elsewhere.
- Everyone on the product team has to learn how to give constructive and meaningful feedback to the designers. Do a Design Review session when you have a new set of designs so you can collect valuable feedback from the team.

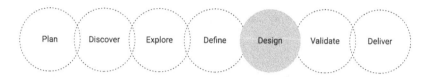

#5 Design

Create The Visual Designs

At this point, we've created the detailed wireframes and conducted usability tests to refine the prototypes. We have all the screens in the wireframes with the layout, copy, and all the elements. It's time to add the visuals so the product can really start to shine.

The goal of the Design phase is to create detailed and pixel-perfect visual designs for the product. Here, we add colors, refined typography, and images, and we put it all together in the final layout. Wireframes don't create emotions in the users. Imagine your house after the drywall is finished. The house is there, and the walls are there, but it's not "home" yet. Visual design is often called UI design (user interface design); these are the final designs that developers will use to code the product.

The visual design is the playground for designers (visual designers, UI designers; it's all the same). It's a different discipline—we would need to add far more pages to this book in order to go into all of the nuts and bolts of how to create visual designs. However, it's a crucial step in the design process. That's why we're going to look at what makes a good visual design and the process you should follow to create detailed visual designs. Let's dive in!

What makes a good visual design?

Before we begin, let's be clear on one thing: The goal of the wireframes was to create the structure and bring in all the elements. That's where we had to decide where to put a certain button or image. Now, during the Design phase, we're going to add more layers. It's important to handle structure and visual design separately. Don't think about colors and visual design when you're doing the wireframes, and don't change the structure or mess around with the elements during the visual design.

From the UX perspective, the design has to be efficient and help the users understand the designs. It's not art; it's craft. We're not using a color because it looks great, we're using it because it works for the particular element or screen. We're not choosing a font because it looks neat, we're choosing it because it's easy to read, works well in different sizes, and appeals to the users.

These five traits have to be followed by visual designers, but it's crucial that everyone on the team knows the principles of a good design. This knowledge will help everyone when it comes to having meaningful discussions on the design and giving feedback to the designers. These principles should be applied to wireframes as well.

Be clear and be consistent!

It's said that good design is invisible. This means it's usable, minimal, and you don't even realize that you're using it to perform a task. The design simply helps you quickly and easily understand how things work. Product design isn't a work of art. It can be beautiful, but the focus is on being usable and useful.

When creating the wireframes, simplicity is important. You should only put the necessary elements on the screen. It's also imperative to take the visitors by the hand and walk them through the process. This can be done with simple, clear interfaces.

Being simple in visual design means that we don't increase the cognitive load of the user. An example of this is using colors for the sole purpose of helping the user navigate and identify the important elements. Adding too much color leads to loss of focus (that is to say, everything looks important, so nothing is important). Simple, clear designs tend to have better conversion and better usability than their visually complex counterparts.

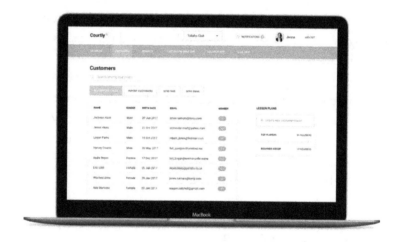

Be simple and clear. Most people think of a clean interface as something that's easy to use.

Another big thing in visual design is consistency. Consistency means that you use the elements the same way every time in a design. For example, when you're using a button with a certain style, you'll use that style across all the designs. Applying consistency makes it easier for the users to understand the design. If they've learned what a button looks like on your website, they shouldn't have to learn it again. Maintaining a consistent design also saves time for developers. Using typography, colors, and elements in the same manner across the designs means less development. Adding new screens is also much easier, and they won't stand out from the "old" ones.

I know consistency can be a challenge for a lot of designers and product companies, but I'll tell you a secret: It just takes time and attention. Take time to review the designs and to check that you've used the elements consistently (buttons, colors, logos, typography, pop-ups, navigation, input fields, success/error messages, labels, etc.).

Apply great visual hierarchy.

Everything is not equal in the visual designs; there are elements that stand out more and draw the attention of the visitors. When you look at a website or mobile app, there are things that you see right away and things you notice later on. Visual hierarchy influences the order in which the human eye perceives a design. What does it see first? What draws your attention? In other words, visual hierarchy is a tool for designers to define what's important in a design and what's not (it's more like a scale than a yes or no question).

Below is a quick example illustrating visual hierarchy. You probably saw "YOUR EYES HERE" first, since it's the biggest and the boldest thing on the page. There's not much text on the page, but since it's much smaller and positioned to the right, "Isn't that fascinating?" doesn't get as much attention.

YOUR EYES HERE

(THEN HERE)

Isn't that **fascinating?**

Playing with size is simple but effective. Visual hierarchy is about creating priorities with sizing, positioning, colors, and whitespace.

There are several factors that influence visual hierarchy, such as size, positioning, and visual style (color, typography, etc.). This brings us to the fact that you begin designing the visual hierarchy when you're creating the wireframes (e.g., creating big bold text for headlines, placing elements in a certain position, and determining what goes where). During the Design phase, the visual hierarchy gets more attention.

Here are a few factors that influence visual hierarchy:

- **Size:**
  Obviously, the bigger an element is, the more attention it gets.
- **Positioning:**
  There's vertical and horizontal prioritization. The higher you place an element, the more attention it gets. Also, there are focus zones and blind spots on a website (check out the famous "F-shaped pattern" of reading the web).
- **Colors:**
  Bright and vivid colors draw attention. Pale colors are less intru-

210

sive. There's also contrast. If you apply high contrast, it draws attention and makes an element of text stand out more.

Use great typography.

Typography includes the choice of fonts, color, size, kerning, and line height between rows. Great typography makes your text easily readable. Remember, people don't read on the web; they scan through the pages. Using different font sizes and formatting (like bold or italics) will make this process easier.

Typography plays an important role in the visual design. Clean sophisticated typography is beautiful. It makes the product look more engaging and of higher quality. It also sets the tone of the designs. Just compare the feeling of the New York Times and its classical serif font with Airbnb's lightweight typography.

Finding the right fonts and designing great typography can be a challenge for visual designers. It takes time and practice to become an expert at this. Typography is not only a question of visual design. There are thousands of websites using light gray text that's barely readable for the majority of people. This brings us to the fact that typography is crucial when it come to the accessibility standpoint.

The text should always be readable!

This is extremely important. No light gray text, please. And no lightweight fonts for non-retina displays. Not everybody has a Mac with a beautiful retina display. Think about poor quality displays and what happens when somebody turns down the brightness on their phone. Gray text becomes unreadable. You always need to apply contrast to make the text clear and keep it easily readable. Sometimes this means it's going to be less fancy, but again, this is not a work of art.

Use whitespace for good.

Apart from size, the amount of space around an element—called whitespace—can also make a difference in visual hierarchy. Giving enough "space" for a headline or a CTA will make it stand out and help the reader scan at the same time.

Don't forget about glyphs.

This one's special. There are languages that require glyphs (e.g., German, Spanish, and Hungarian).

Use colors and contrast properly.

Color theory is another big deal in visual design, but the basics are simple. We have a hierarchy here as well. The brighter and more vivid a color is, the more attention it gets. There are colors that tend to have more impact, too. For example, multiple tests have shown that one of the best converting CTA colors is orange. Now, don't go running to your designs and changing the color to orange; just make a mental note of this. Orange is vivid, bright, saturated, and has a slight "caution" feel (just like red does).

Colors create emotions in us, so there's a psychology to colors as well. Interestingly, the impact and perception of a color is very different across different cultures.

In Western culture, white represents purity, cleanness, and safety. In Far Eastern culture, white is the color of mourning.

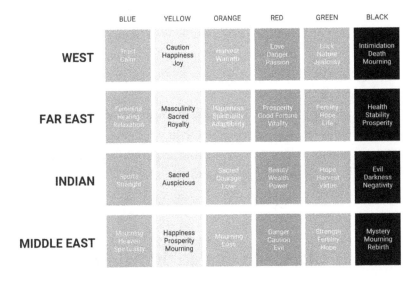

This chart shows how each color is perceived in different cultures. You have to know the market and the culture you're targeting.

Here are some tips on using colors:

- Always have a main color. This is the strongest and most important color that dominates the design. Use the main color for the most important interactions (e.g., CTA buttons). Don't use more than two or three strong colors.
- Play around with saturation! More important elements should be more vivid.
- Understand how a color will be perceived by the target users. Learn about the emotions color and design create in them. What associations do they have? Or the other way around: What colors

would they connect to your brand? You can use five-second tests and usability tests to understand this impact (this is covered in the next chapter).

- Use contrast when you want to draw the visitors' attention. For example, applying high contrast on your homepage can make it look catchy. However, on a shopping cart page, the layout should be bright and clean, and the text should be the only thing with contrast.
- Learn the basics of color theory. Learn about primary, secondary, complementary, and triadic colors as well as how to create monochromatic colors. A great way to start playing around with colors is to use Coolors. It's online and free; you'll also find a lot of premade color themes to use in your designs there.

Start with design principles.

Before you jump into the visual designs, you have to decide what you want to achieve with the visuality. What kind of feelings and emotions do you want to create in the users? Should the design be sophisticated or simple? Do you want it to feel more luxurious or more affordable? It's crucial to tie down these goals and create principles for the design.

So, before you start the visual design, sit down with your team and brainstorm what you want to achieve. There are two techniques you can use to come up with the principles for the design:

- Use a spectrum of attributes to get started.
- Come up with five adjectives that will reflect the designs.

Use a spectrum of attributes to get started.

The easiest way to get started is to use a spectrum of attributes. The spectrum lists a couple of opposing attributes like "expensive" and "affordable." You have to decide where to place the design on the spectrum (it's like the Likert scale).

In the *7STEPUX® Resource Center* you can find a template called the Design Questionnaire for both the spectrum and the adjectives. Feel free to add attributes to the spectrum that better cover your project.

The Design Questionnaire. This is a good way to set principles for the designs. Use the spectrum of attributes and add adjectives that the designs should reflect.

Come up with five adjectives.

The adjectives should convey the most important aspects that the design needs to reflect; for example, "easy-to-use," "friendly," "professional," "trustworthy," and so on.

Come up with a lot of adjectives with your team and choose the five that best describe what you want to achieve with the designs.

Working with clients

If you're working with clients, this step is crucial. If you miss this step, you'll end up guessing what the client wants to see, and you'll come up with designs that are not quite right. Brainstorming and having a solid foundation for design will give you input for the designs. You'll know what to design, and once you have this, you can discuss whether you've successfully fulfilled the principles or if there's room for improvement.

The final look of the design principles. This is a simple way to show what we want to achieve during the design process.

Put it on the wall.

I use the Design Questionnaire in my projects. When I'm finished and have all the inputs, I like to create a final version that displays the principles for the design. I can print this out and put it on the wall for the whole team to see. You can find a template for this in the *7STEPUX® Resource Center*.

Creating "Look and Feel" designs

When starting to create the visual designs, it's best to experiment with multiple design variations and choose the one that best suits the project and design principles. To do this, we're going to create the so-called "Look and Feel" designs. Sometimes, it won't be the first design you create that's the winner.

The idea is simple. You take a wireframe and create two to three visual design concepts. It's best to select a page that's complex and shows the frequently used elements (e.g., the header). For a website, take the homepage and create two to three different design concepts. Each of the designs should align with the design principles, but have a different take on design—different colors, typography, images, and layout. The goal is to create contrast and see which design suits the principles best. This allows us to come up with the desired feel for the users.

Below, you'll find an example of a "Look and Feel" session. There's the wireframe of the screen and three different design concepts. All of them follow the same structure, but they provoke different feelings.

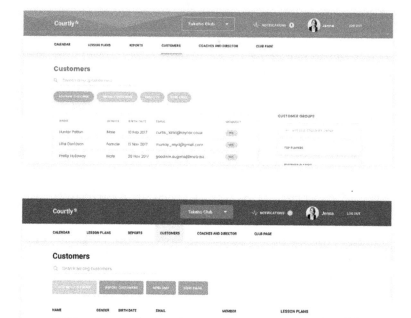

Different design concepts for the same screen. It's worth experimenting to find the best fit for the product before moving on to iterating the designs.

When you have your "Look and Feel" designs, show them to the team, stakeholders, or client. You can even run an interview or five-second test to see which design the users prefer. The goal is to select the design concept you'll flesh out and iterate all the screens based on it.

Tips for creating better "Look and Feel" designs

Start early.

You can start working on the "Look and Feel" designs once you have your first sketches. You don't have to design the final screen—just find a concept that works for the product. If you start creating "Look and Feel" de-

218

signs during the wireframing, you'll have time to experiment and it won't extend the project timeline.

Get inspired.
Before you begin, go ahead and collect some inspiration. There are tons of beautiful designs for every industry on Pinterest, Dribbble, and Behance. Search and collect designs that align nicely with your design principles.

Do at least three variations.
I know it can be a challenge, but try for at least three different design concepts. It's best if they're done by multiple designers, since they'll naturally create different designs. The goal is to have diverse design concepts. Don't just change a color or the typography; redo it completely so it will have a different feeling.

Design systems

One of the biggest challenges of product design is maintaining consistency. Be consistent with colors, typography, and components (buttons, headers, icons, etc.). Consistency is key for a number of reasons. From the users' point-of-view, consistency helps them quickly understand what's happening on the screen. If you have a green "add button" with a plus sign, you should use the exact same design whenever the user needs to add something to the page. Once the user learns that the green button with the plus sign adds something, they'll remember it the next time. This saves time for them and clears up confusion.

A design system is an inventory of all the components, icons, colors, and typography used in the designs. In the past, it was difficult for designers to create and maintain a design system. Interestingly, the concepts and the foundation for the design system came from development; there was a need for developers to be able to think in a system of colors and components as opposed to coding individual screens. A core development principle is to write reusable and flexible code. This means that developers try to think in systems and reuse a piece of code, a CSS class, a function, or a layout whenever they can. This saves time, makes the code cleaner, and saves tons of resources. All the tools are available to do this on the design side of things, too!

- Design system thinking has lots of advantages:
- It makes the designs look very consistent and clean.
- Updating styles is easy and happens across the board. For example, you might need to change the color of your main button. Without a design system, you would need to go through all the designs and replace every instance of that button. With a design system, you simply update the corresponding component.
- A design system addresses use cases that are typically not addressed by the designs. For example, every state of an input field and buttons, including validation errors and mouse states—it's all in there in an easy to use catalog. Other examples include toasts, messages, and modal usage.
- A design system makes it easy for multiple designers to collaborate on the designs and speed up the process by making sure whatever is built is consistent with the rest of the product.
- One of the biggest advantages is, of course, supporting developers in their work. Using a design system, developers can follow their own workflow when creating components, defining styles, and putting together screens without having to worry about any local tweaks or changes to the design. Just imagine it! In the first case, you have a hundred screens to look through. You need to investigate each screen and each element on every screen to make sure you implement the designs as the designer imagined it. You can

see patterns and elements that are used on multiple screens, but you can't be sure, and you always need to double check and make adjustments individually to match the designs. In the second case, you have the design system, and you already know the components that are used in the designs—you have the building blocks. You know that if you see a button or a pop-up in the designs, it will be the same as in the design system. You don't need to worry about individual screens. Instead, you just build the components and put them together. Sounds a lot easier than the first version, right?

What goes into a design system?

Before we discuss the different elements to include in the design system, I want to introduce you to an important and useful design concept: atomic design. Brad Frost published a book under this title that lays out the concept and help designers and teams adopt this methodology. But what's the methodology about? Atomic design is a specific way to build design systems. It has five levels:

- Atoms
- Molecules
- Organisms
- Templates
- Pages

Atoms are components that can't be broken down any further. For example, an atom is a button or a checkbox. Yeah, I know, technically you could break a button down into a label and background shape, but it doesn't make sense to do this because it's not usable like that. So, atoms are the smallest usable elements of the designs.

Some typical examples of atoms are

- Buttons
- Checkboxes
- Radio buttons
- Input fields
- Menu items
- Sliders

Buttons

Atoms are the smallest usable elements of the designs.

Atoms can form molecules. Let's say you're designing a checkbox—that's your atom. Often, you'll pair the checkbox with a label and use them together. You can create a molecule that includes your checkbox and the label. Here are some examples of molecules:

- Search bar (using an input atom and a button atom)
- Save and cancel buttons (these are often used together—make them into a molecule!)
- Checkbox and label; radio button and label

Example of an atom and molecule.

Organisms are formed from molecules—adding another layer of complexity. It can become very exciting at this point! Organisms are extremely valuable and reusable components. Here are some examples of organisms:

- Pop-ups; modals
- Success messages
- Headers; footers
- Dropdown menus

Organism examples.

The next level is templates. A template is made by grouping organisms together. This is when the screen of a website or application starts to make sense. Basically, templates are pages without real content. For example, if you have a blog, you have a template for the article page. Every article that appears on your blog will use the same template. Next, there's the pages level, the final design. Pages are actual screens with real content.

Let's go back to our original question: What goes into the design system? The reason I introduced the atomic design approach is because it's a good way to think about the components that form the system. As with everything, though, you need to be flexible! You can adopt atomic design and build design systems even if you don't strictly follow the levels above.

In addition, you need to be aware that you'll have different numbers of components for each level. What do I mean by this? You'll likely have quite a few atoms, as they're very fundamental to the design. In my experience though, you'll probably have significantly fewer molecules, and that's okay! You only need to build molecules (and components from other levels) if you're going to want to reuse them later. Moving forward, organisms are very frequently used—just think of all the examples of pop-ups, headers, and footers we talked about. Then there's the templates and pages levels, which are merged in a lot of cases. Do you want to omit templates and put together screens (aka pages) using the components you've built? That's perfectly fine, and it works! You don't have to use all the levels, and you don't have to create components from everything in the designs.

Design system creation 101

When is it a good time to start building your design system? That's an easy one: Start building it during the Design phase (aka UI design). There's no need to work with a design system when you're creating wireframes. Don't slow the process down! Remember, the Explore and Define chapters were all about designing the architecture of the website or application. You can also skip design systems when doing "Look and Feel" designs. The reason for this is super simple: Why create a system for multiple design concepts before you know which direction you're headed? In other words, the perfect moment to build your design system is when you have your wireframes ready and the "Look and Feel" design you want to go with. Let's go back to the basics and see exactly what you need to include in a design system. I'll use a web application as an example. There are two fundamental parts of the system that I like to create first:

- Colors
- Typography

Some designers dive into creating screens using colors, and on the way, a color palette begins to form. Near the end of the project, when the designs are handed over to the developers, is when the designer finalizes the colors used in the app. Inevitably, following this process will lead to lots of inconsistencies and, eventually, more work for the designer who needs to keep the screens consistent. I recommend creating the color palette as one of the first steps when creating the design system. Take the "Look and Feel" design and map out all the colors you're going to need. Think through the use cases of the colors.

- Colors for validation (error or success states and messages)
- Lighter, softer colors for dividers, drop shadows, and outlines
- Colors for disabled states and less prominent elements on the screen

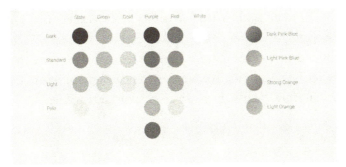

This is a color palette I designed for a sudoku app called Brainsword.

225

You want to do the same thing with typography. Using the "Look and Feel" design, break the typography down and define styles for each use case.

Heading 1 Bold (28 pt)   Heading 1 SemiBold (28 pt)

Heading 2 Bold (26 pt)   Heading 2 SemiBold (26 pt)

Heading 3 Bold (24 pt)   Heading 3 SemiBold (24 pt)

Heading 4 (22 pt)   Heading 4 Semibold(22 pt)

Heading 5 (20 pt)   Heading 5 Semibold(20 pt)

Text 1 Regular (18 pt)	Text 1 SemiBold (18 pt)	**Text 1 Bold (18 pt)**
Text 2 Regular (16 pt)	Text 2 SemiBold (16 pt)	**Text 2 Bold (16 pt)**
Text 3 Regular (14 pt)	Text 3 SemiBold (14 pt)	**Text 3 Bold (14 pt)**
Text 4 Regular (12 pt)	Text 4 SemiBold (12 pt)	**Text 4 Bold (12 pt)**

Creating styles for typography makes the life of the designer and developer so much easier.

When you're done with the colors and typography, it's time to move on to components. This is when you need to put your atomic design hat on and start to think about atoms, molecules, and organisms. Building the design system and creating the actual screens is a continuous process that goes hand in hand. When you design a new element that's not part of the design system, you need to make a decision whether to include the element in the system or not. And guess what, you don't have to include everything. If you only use a certain design element once, what's the point of including it in the design system and making it reusable?

The criticism of design systems and what to do about it

There's a pitfall to design systems that you want to avoid—sacrificing user experience for uniformity. This issue can surface later on with a more mature and extensive design system. At first, everyone loves the idea of making things consistent. It makes the designer's life easier, improves UX, makes the developers happier, and makes development way more efficient, which directly affects the bottom line. After a while, designers can get lazy, or they're required to always work from the available components from the design system and the focus slowly shifts from designing and building the ideal solution to building the easiest solution. Maybe the designer wants to design a new component but product management decides to go with the existing component because it's already built (so why use the precious development resources on this?).

Working with a design system also requires a higher level of skills and experience from a designer. I'm not saying beginner designers shouldn't use design systems. But there have been many times I've seen junior designers working with design systems in which they just used whatever was in the inventory and didn't ask questions like, "Does this component work here?" and "Is this a good solution, or do we need something else?" Design systems should evolve with the product This means there's a need for finding new solutions and getting rid of the ones that don't work.

Luckily, there's an easy solution to this problem, which lies in the workflow. Many designers skip the sketching and wireframing part when they're working with a design system. Let's say you're a designer working on an existing product and you need to design a new feature. All the elements and assets are at your fingertips. Why go back and create wireframes when you can build final designs instead? This is a trick question! Don't fall for it! Even though I have tons of experience, I still always do sketching and/or wireframing. Why? Because the point of the sketching and wireframing is to allow your mind to focus on the ideal solution without having to worry about components, design systems, and what's feasible for development. When you have a good design system, it's vital to create sketches and wireframes before you create visual designs.

Creating wireframes first will allow you to circumvent the design system during your brainstorming so that you can come up with a genuine, spot-on solution to the problem you're trying to solve. Once you have the ideal solution in your wireframes, you can open the discussion up around how to implement it using the design system. This is an awesome workflow because it lets you make a well-informed decision.

- You have the ideal solution for the problem in your wireframes
- You see what's possible with the design system and what's (currently) not
- You can discuss with developers whether to implement changes in the design system, implement the designs individually or revert back to using a component from the design system.

The last point is extremely important. Design decisions should be influenced by three factors: the users' point-of-view (UX), the business goals, and the technical feasibility. At the end of the day, it's going to be a business decision. Maybe the particular problem you're trying to solve isn't important from the user or business point of view, so there's no harm in using a less "perfect" solution from the design system because you win more with the time saved on development. In other cases, you'll want to adjust the design system and add to it because it's so important that it's worth the time. All in all, following this workflow will ensure that you'll make the right decision.

Tools for building design systems

This is a good news/bad news situation. The bad news is that you can't build a design system with just any design tool. Practically, you're limited to just a few. The good news is that there's software that we already talked about that checks all the boxes, works on every platform, and makes collaboration easy—Figma. Figma is the only tool that can help you build and scale a design system without having to subscribe to other tools. There's Sketch and Adobe XD as the other big shots in this arena, but they're a bit of a bumpy ride, and you need other tools like Zeplin and InVision to make up for the functionality that Figma offers. If you're serious about design systems and want to give it a try, Figma is free, so you have nothing to lose.

Style guides versus design systems

I mention style guides here and there, and in the earlier editions of this book there was even more discussion around style guides. Style guides are a collection of frequently used design elements, and they also feature the colors and typography used in the designs. There's a big difference between design systems and style guides though—design systems are built by designers for designers and developers, while styles guides are meant for a broader audience. Style guides are accessible to anybody in the company (e.g., management, marketing, and HR). Brand assets, voice, and tone are often included in style guides, making them a go-to document about the brand (they also include visuals, of course). Here's what goes into a style guide versus a design system:

Style guide	Design system
Logo usage	Colors used in the designs
Brand colors	Typography used in the designs
Typography	Frequently reused components
Voice and tone	Can also include the elements of a style guide
Guidelines for illustrations, pictures, icons, or any imagery used by the brand	
High-level directions for product design	

Continue iterating the design.

After you have the winning "Look and Feel," it's time to create the detailed pixel-perfect visual design for all of the screens. This is where the visual designers spend most of their time and work hard on creating every screen. The goal here is to think of every possible screen, element, and state that will be used during the development.

In addition to the screens, think about...

Different states of the elements

What happens if the users hover over a button? How can you display that a button is disabled? You have to design for every possible interaction.

If not, the developers are going to ask for it, and if they don't, there will be a piece missing from your puzzle.

Pop-ups, modals, and tooltips

How do you display system messages? Can you delete something in the product? If so, you need to have a way to confirm the deletion. It's important to design these interfaces as well. Why? They almost look the same! Isn't it enough to just design one? Well, in my experience, the best approach is to think about it like a designer. It might be that the only difference between two pop-ups is the text, but remember the microcopy. It has to be written! If you leave it out, you won't know there's copy to be written. What's more, the more precise and thorough you are in iterating the designs, the more time you save for the developers.

Onboarding

Onboarding is another part of UX. In essence, onboarding is the process of welcoming the users when they first start using the product. It's the first-time user experience. I'm not talking about those shitty tooltips on a transparent black background with arrows pointing to every corner on the screen. hat's bad practice and doesn't make sense. Let me tell you why. When you buy a tool, I bet you don't read the manual first. I bet you try to figure out how to use it on your own. Maybe you struggle with it, but this is how most of us operate. We might refer to the manual later if we can't figure out how the tool works on our own, but it's not our first go-to.

The same thing applies in the digital world. First, you have to let the users explore your product; the product has to be self-explanatory.

231

Don't design a crappy interface that's barely understandable and then try to find ways to explain how it works. Design a better interface. Do as much as you can to create a great and easy-to-understand product. But, in some cases, this is not enough. This is when onboarding comes in. For example, you have to set up and add a few details before you start using a tool. Alternatively, the tool is simple, but the users have to understand a few things first. Once they get it, it's a piece of cake. This is when a smart onboarding process can help you out.

The following are some practices to avoid:

- Crappy arrows pointing to every corner of the screen in front of a transparent black background (I know you've seen this at least once)
- Forcing users to refer to tutorial videos to figure out how the product works (or even worse, making them read something)
- Putting pop-ups everywhere

Let me expand on the last point. I'm not saying pop-ups are bad, but be aware that people love to ignore pop-ups. It's like developing banner blindness. See a pop-up? Closed in one second. The problem with pop-ups is that, most of the time, we see one of two types: (1) success, error, or technical messages or (2) ads. Think about this when creating a pop-up. You don't want to fall into either of these categories. Instead, go full screen and try to grab the attention of the users. Create an anti-pop-up. Here's what you should do:

Be self-explanatory.

Designing an interface that explains itself isn't easy, especially if the product is complex and has a lot of functionality. Thinking about flows first will help a lot. I also have to mention microcopy again. Sometimes a better name for a function or a button will solve the problem. Writing better instructions and better error and success messages is also helpful. Better input labels and placeholders make it easier for users to understand what's going on. Don't create pop-ups and tooltips for onboarding until you've made sure the microcopy is great.

Create smart empty states.

One of the most powerful tools are the so-called empty states. An empty state is what you show to the users when you have no data because they haven't started using the product yet (they haven't created a list, added a profile, added to-dos, etc.). Instead of leaving a screen empty, we can use that space to draw the visitors' attention and show them what to do.

This is an excellent example of an empty screen. There's no food added, but instead of a blank screen, you can see that your meals will appear once you start adding them, and it shows you how to get started.

A good example of an empty state screen is one that has no data but allows you to see what to do next (e.g., installation instructions). This is an opportunity to add a bit of personality and build engagement with the users. Adding a nice illustration and optimized microcopy will enhance the user experience.

Call attention to important elements with tooltips.

Adding a nice tooltip and showing the users exactly what to do and where to find something can be great practice too. Just make sure you don't overdo it (one tooltip at a time, please!), and make sure the tooltip looks engaging. This is a must; otherwise, you'll get the banner blindness effect again.

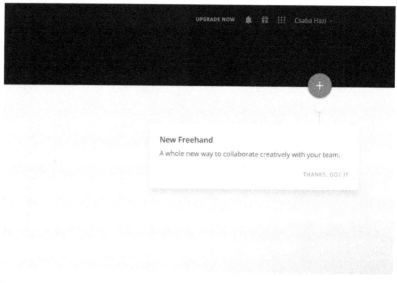

Use tooltips to draw users' attention to important elements on the screen. They're powerful, but be careful; don't overdo it!

Step by step

Like I said, there are cases where the users need to go through a set up process before accessing the tool. They have to set up their account, install a tracking a code, enter their preferences, and so on. The goal here is to minimize the amount of information that we ask for from the users. Remember, they want to get in as fast as possible. My first suggestion is that you always ask yourself if you really need to ask for a piece of information and, if so, if you could ask for it later on.

The other important thing is to break down and create a process instead of asking for all the information up front. Despite the common myth that users don't like to click, the reality is that what users truly hate is when they're forced to enter a lot of information on an overwhelming interface. If you break the information down into chunks, you can take the user by the hand and enable them to quickly enter bits of information. It all comes down to making it feel easy. If something looks easy to do, we're more likely to do it. And if something looks frighteningly complex, we tend to abandon it.

Duolingo is great at making an otherwise boring process fun, such as when signing up or entering your preferences. I started learning High Valyrian.

Duolingo is a great example. Obviously, before you can get started, you need to enter information about yourself and your current knowledge level. However, this feels easy to do because it's broken down into small steps. You always know what to do, and every step takes only a few seconds.

Let me skip it

When it comes to onboarding, you have to let the users skip it. If you create smart and engaging onboarding, there will be users who complete it. However, there will always be people who want to get in and start to play around with the product right away. This is why creating a self-explanatory design is essential.

Internal notifications and error handling

Do you have designs for the 404, 403, and 500 error messages? Well, you should. Obviously you want to avoid a situation when a user clicks on a dead link, but shit happens. The question is, are you prepared for this situation or not?

If users arrive on a 404 page, it's a low point in their journey. They wanted to do or see something, but they won't, because it's missing. Therefore, you have to think like a smart customer service rep and do your best to get the users back on track again. Designing error pages is crucial. You have to explain to the users what happened and give options on how to move forward; otherwise, you risk losing them.

The same thing applies to error handling. Think of a CRM system where you can add new profiles and edit and save them. What happens if the connection breaks down and the users enter the wrong information or there's an internal technical issue? In all cases, you have to inform the users (hello, microcopy!) so they understand what happened, and you have to give them hints on how they can solve the problem or what they can do instead.

Design for mobile devices

Let's talk about mobile for a bit since we have to design for mobile devices differently than for desktop devices (e.g., laptops and PCs). When you have to design for both platforms, it's best to design them separately. Since usage tends to shift from desktop to mobile devices, in most cases, it's a wise move to think mobile first. Let's look at the difference between designing for mobile devices and desktop.

You can see that there are more differences between these platforms than just the screen size. You have to consider all of these aspects when designing for mobile devices (be it for a mobile app or a responsive web design).

Mobile devices	Desktop
We use our hands to tap on the interface. All the elements should be easily reachable and big enough to tap on easily.	We use a mouse or touchpad to control the device. The clicks are more precise with a mouse, so smaller elements can also work well on the screen.

Mobile devices	Desktop
There's no hover state (when you hover your mouse over an element), but the screen can be pressure sensitive (with some devices).	There's more screen real estate.
You can use gestures (swiping, pushing, shaking) to control the device.	There are no gestures, but you can use the right-click function of the mouse.
The keyboard is not always accessible, and it's not convenient to type a lot on mobile. You have to minimize the amount of information the user needs to enter.	We can type easily with a keyboard and use it for commands and shortcuts.
It's used under various conditions like on the way to the office or at home. It's often used in a noisy environment full of distractions.	It's mostly used in a calm environment like the office or at home.
The screen real estate is very limited.	There's more screen real estate to work with.
Not all parts of the screen are easy to reach. With a screen size over 4.5 inches, the upper corners are out of reach.	All parts of the screen are easy to reach with the mouse and touchpad.

To hold or not to hold? That is the question.

Unlike desktop computers, we have to hold mobile devices. This brings us to an issue where not all parts of the screen are easily reachable. Usually (49% of the time), people hold the phone in one hand. This means they can only use one finger to control the phone and, when it comes to a screen larger than 4.5 inches, the upper areas of the screen become difficult to reach. From the design standpoint, this is the most difficult position to design for.

The second most frequent position is holding the phone with one hand and using the free hand to tap on it. This is especially true for larger phones that are easy to drop when being held with just one hand.

Finally, the third most frequently used hand position is holding the phone with both hands. This grip enables the user to reach the middle and bottom of the screen easily without stretching their fingers.

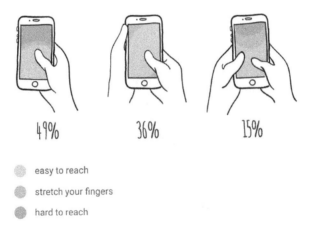

- easy to reach
- stretch your fingers
- hard to reach

This chart shows how most people hold their phones. You can see which areas are easy to reach and which areas are difficult.

Most people use their phones with one hand. In the above image, you can see which parts of the screen are easy to reach and which parts are hard to reach. Green is easy, orange is not very comfortable, and red is "Ouch!" If you examine the one-handed position you can see that the upper areas are only accessible by changing grip. Why should we care about this?

Most applications use the upper ("header") area for placing navigation and other important elements. This creates a problem for the 49% of users who are using their phones with one hand. This is well above a certain device and hand size, obviously, but I wouldn't go optimizing the screen for Rachmaninoff's hand.

How do you design with hand positions in mind?

You have to always keep in mind how people will use, hold, and tap on a device. Limitations mean that we have to prioritize. You have to decide how important an element is and how often users will use it. This will tell you how accessible the element should be.

Position the most used and important elements on the screen so they are easily accessible. As a rule of thumb, the navigation and the CTA should always be easy to reach and tap. Even though people are five times more likely to abandon sites that are poorly optimized for mobile, a lot of apps and responsive websites don't follow this rule.

Always check your designs on mobile.

When you design for mobile devices (meaning tablets, phones, and wearables) the number one rule is to check it on the actual device users are going to use it on. Why? Because if you don't hold the device in your hand, it's easy to forget about hand positions and what's easy or difficult to reach on the screen. As you design, you have to immediately check whether the mobile design is easy and convenient to use or if it has to be adjusted.

Most designs are done on a desktop device, and there's nothing wrong with that. But, it's a different situation. You have a big screen that's further away from you, a keyboard, and a mouse. It's difficult to get the sizes right for the text and elements—this is why you have to check it on the mobile device.

It's best to start doing this when creating the digital wireframes. Pick a tool that easily lets you mirror the designs and preview them on a mobile device. This will help you design better elements, avoid text size that's too big or too small, and use the space wisely.

Sketch offers a mobile app called Sketch Mirror, which will show the designs on your mobile; you can follow the changes in real time. Figma has a similar app called Figma Mirror.

More and more tools offer the live preview functionality. Both Figma and Sketch have an app that you can download to your phone and see the changes in the designs in real-time without having to sync or upload the designs. Photoshop has a similar solution called Device Preview. These tools are incredible help during the wireframing and visual design. You can check if you get the size right for the elements, play around with the whitespace as well as font-sizes to see what can fit on a screen. In fact, it's nuts to design without this preview.

Mobile designs should be tested on mobile devices.

This might sound like a no-brainer, but I've seen people test mobile designs on laptops. This is even true for people presenting to other team members and stakeholders. But the experience isn't the same. If you're designing for mobile phones, you should show it and test it on a phone. If it's for a tablet, show it and test it on a tablet.

Content is just as important as visual design.

In the Design phase, there are more things than just the design to take care of.

- We have to write the final copy.
- We have to refine and finalize the microcopy.
- We have to add images, videos, and other visual content to the designs.
- We have to add transitions and animations to help users understand how the product works and to enhance the user experience.

Content is just as important as the visual design itself. If you have a great design, but your content sucks, users will dump your product. I've often been asked, "What kind of content should I show to visitors?" Since you have a wide range of tools for content like text, images, videos, slideshows, user-generated content, interactive content and so on, answering this question is most important for websites and products that work with content. To answer this question, you have to ask yourself these five questions:

- **Who** is the content for?
- **Where** will the users see it?
- **When** will the users see it?
- **Why** is it important to the users?
- **How** should you display the content?

Copywriting is an essential part of UX.

Ideally, you started writing the labeling copy when creating the wireframes. In the Design phase, it's best to write the final copy so you have the full picture of the product with the final design and final copy.

When doing the copywriting, make sure you follow these guidelines:

Make the copy informative.

Whether it's a headline or a product description, it has to add value to the users. Remember that people don't really want to read on the web, they want information ASAP. This means you have to condense the communication and focus on what's really important. Bill Beard said, "The best experiences have minimal copy because they're intuitive."

Use the right jargon.

One of the top problems I've seen on websites is that they use jargon that users don't understand. This can be a deal-breaking issue. You have to explore and understand the jargon that users are familiar with (using, for example, a usability test or user interview) and make sure that you use phrases they understand.

Go for emotions and be persuasive.

Good copy is not just informative; it's also persuasive. It persuades the users to follow the process, buy a product, and/or read or watch content. Good copy will convert the visitors into customers. Emotions are also crucial in marketing communication. Remember the fears and goals in our persona templates? Addressing fears in your marketing communication will help the users bypass those fears and take the next step. Reinforcing that you understand and support their goals will help build engagement between you and your users.

Encourage users to take action.

Great copy will tell users exactly what to do (e.g., buy the product, use feature x, consume content, or share something on social media). You have to be explicit and straightforward.

The impact of great microcopy

We already discussed microcopy in the Define chapter. Microcopy is some of the most impactful content. Microcopy helps users understand the product and has a direct impact on the conversions and engagement of the users. Improving microcopy alone can lead to a huge increase in conversions.

Microcopy can be written in no time, and you can easily test its impact. During a usability test (more on this in the next chapter), pay extra attention to microcopy. Likewise, doing an A/B test to fine tune the microcopy can show everybody on the team how huge of an impact these small gains can have.

A picture is worth a thousand words.

Sixty-five percent of the population are visual learners. This is fascinating, since the human mind can process visual information 60,000 times as fast as written text.

But there's more:

- Fifty percent of your brain works on processing visual information.
- Of the total amount of receptors in your body, 70% are in your eyes.
- You can process an image in a tenth of a second.

Nowadays, products are becoming increasingly visual. Look at Instagram, Pinterest, and Snapchat, and you'll see that they mainly operate with pictures and videos. Facebook is also putting more emphasis on visual content by using larger images, ranking visual content higher in the feed, displaying text as images with colored backgrounds, and so on. Unlike text, images are easy to understand, and they instantly create associations and feelings in our minds.

For example, in this image (which could be a section on a homepage), the background helps you understand the context of the design and figure out what it's all about before reading the text. The colors and visual layout create associations and emotions. In this case, the soft earth tones and the image create the relaxed and cozy feeling of home.

Images help users understand what a site or interface is about.

Using pictures the right way will help users understand what the product or content is about. Think of pictures as shortcuts to the users' minds. Use the visual processing power of the brain to illustrate and explain through pictures.

Here are some tips for using images better:

Always use pictures with a purpose.

Pictures, illustrations, infographics, and images are great, but you always have to use them with a purpose. Don't just insert an image in the design because it looks good. Think of an image as a piece of content. The image can serve a decorative purpose to enhance the design (like a background image), but it has to resonate with the content and add value to the design.

Check readability.
A common design problem is when the designers place text on the images and it becomes unreadable. This is bad for both the text and the image. As a rule of thumb, always make sure that all text is easy to read—this is the number one priority. There are several techniques for placing text on images and maintaining readability.

Match up the style of the images with the design.
When you think of images as pieces of content, you'll want them in the same style as your text and other design elements. Remember, the images need to reflect the content.

Go for high quality.
Always use high-quality, relevant photos. They also have to be credible to the users. For example, don't put a photo of a delicious looking cheeseburger on your site when you only have lousy sandwiches to sell. People want to see what they're going to get—it can be a product, a licensed tool, downloadable material, or anything. You have to present it with the best possible packaging, but always remain credible.

Dump stock photos.
People can tell if you're using stock photos (in this case, I mean bad stock photos). These are the photos that are too good to be true, showing unbelievably perfect people with perfect lighting and unnatural gestures.

You can be sure it's a stock photo if

- it looks artificial or unnatural (look at that alien smile!),
- it's too perfect (in which case, it's gotta be Photoshopped), and/or
- its shows fake emotions and gestures (people are very good at identifying real versus fake emotions).

The problem with stock photos is that they can backfire; people can see that they're not real. Just look at this picture below:

My ALL-TIME-FAVORITE. I have nothing to add to this image. Nothing.

This is one of my favorite stock photos ever. It seems this lady has no idea how to hold a hammer; it's impossible to hammer the laptop this way since her left elbow is on the table. Fortunately, we can see her face, which is the most unnatural angry face ever. Actually, this would make a great emoticon. And you know what's funny? I paid 33 bucks to show this to you. I'm insane.

Whenever you can, make sure you avoid using stock photos. Especially avoid the ones that show an unnatural and unreal situation, such as the one above. Of course, there are rare cases when you need to have a photo of something special. Several years ago, I was working on a landing page for a driving school. They had special training for using forklifts. Obviously, it was a special case. The company didn't have photos of the forklifts, so we had to download some good photos from a stock photo website. Aside from that situation, I've never had to use them again.

There are, however, a growing number of free stock photo sites that offer royalty free, high-quality photos that you can use in your designs. They're not artificial looking. In fact, they're beautiful. They're mostly useful for a great background. Check out Pexels.com and Unsplash.com.

A video is worth a thousand pictures.

People are spending more and more time watching videos. Videos are becoming a major part of our decision-making process when we buy something. According to a survey, videos help 73% of people make a purchase decision.

Videos are engaging. In addition, they can explain how a product, service, or function works. Videos can use a wide range of tools, such as animation, real footage, music, voiceovers, and text. There are a lot of startups that have validated whether there was a need for their product with a video before creating the product itself. A famous example is Dropbox. They created a video showing how their product worked and collected subscribers. Since it was a great success, they decided to develop the actual product.

Videos come in all shapes and sizes (e.g., an educational video showing how to use the product, a promotional video pitching the product, a background video enhancing the design, or something created for brand awareness).

The effect is similar to using images, but videos are much more powerful because

- there's more time to present an idea or product,
- a video background can create a strong atmosphere, and
- users can get the most out of the product by watching tutorial videos.

Prioritize!

UX is about prioritization, and content is no exception. Below, you'll see a chart showing how much impact each content type has on the user experience as well as how much time and energy each one takes to create. From this, you can choose which content type would best suit your needs and budget. Microcopy is the all-time winner, of course, since it has a huge impact on the experience and is quick and easy to create. Remember, not focusing on microcopy is Not an option! And, using great images and illustrations on your website and app will ease the users' path to understanding the product—building engagement and credibility. Just follow the guidelines we discussed!

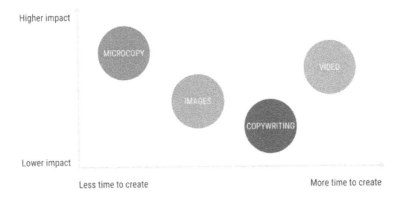

This chart shows the impact on the perception of an interface of each content type.

Design Prototypes and high-fidelity prototypes

As with wireframes, we need to create a click-through prototype from the visual design. We have the final pixel-perfect layout, and this is where we give it some feeling. Remember that despite best intentions, some stakeholders will only be able to understand the product when they can sit down and click through the final design. Design prototypes are also important for developers. They allow developers to try a product to see how it should work (and to learn which screens are linked together). This way, designers aren't just handing off designs and assets for development.

So far, we've only covered click-through prototypes. These are great and helpful most of the time. However, there are cases when you need more— you need to see how an animation or transition between screens would work or how a complex feature would work that can't be shown with the click-through prototype (e.g., a chatbot). This is when you need a high-fidelity prototype.

High-fidelity prototypes look and behave almost like the living product. They can show a complex feature, animations, transitions using gestures, and much more. Currently, the compromise is that they're great for showing one function or displaying one set of animations, but they're not able to show dozens of screens like click-through prototypes are.

What are high-fidelity prototypes good for?

Showing complex animations

With high-fidelity prototypes, you can model every sort of animation and transition (e.g., you click on a button, and it expands to fill the whole screen with a color that pushes the other elements off the screen and shows something new). High-fidelity prototypes are great to experiment with and allow us to show our ideas to the team and the developers (who will create the animations and transitions for the living product).

Showing how a single feature works

Sometimes click-through isn't enough when you need to work with data or you want to show a set of interactions (and not just one at a time like in a click-thru). For example, you can model a chatbot where you enter the message which is then displayed on the screen, and the bot replies or uses the mobile phone camera to capture photos and edit them. It's great to play around with different solutions and try out a function before developing it.

Remember, it's all about saving time.

I have two pieces of advice for you. The first is to think of a high-fidelity prototype as a tool for experimenting. It's not designed (yet) to show a full-blown product, but static designs are very limited, and sometimes you need to see it "live" to decide whether what you imagined really works. The second is that you remember that prototypes are meant to save you time. If it takes too long, it's not worth it (remember, you're going to throw it away after using it). In this case, it's better to get your product done using fewer functions in order to allow you to test out the critical parts.

With all this in mind, there are three cases in which you might want to use a high-fidelity prototype:

- If you can't show how the function works with a click-thru prototype
- If development is taking too much time and you want to show it to the users
- If you want to show a feature, an animation, or a transition to the developers and see what they can make of it without giving them instructions

There's a big difference between click-through prototypes and high-fidelity prototypes. In a click-through prototype, you only work with images. In a high-fidelity prototype, you can work with every layer in the design separately (shapes, forms, buttons, and texts). This allows you to create sophisticated animations and transitions between the screens.

Here are a few high-fidelity prototyping tools worth checking out:

Proto.io

Proto.io is a cloud-based tool, so it runs in your browser. You can easily import designs from Sketch or build up a design with their built-in elements. You can also work with data (e.g., add an input field that users can actually fill in), then work with the data they entered later.

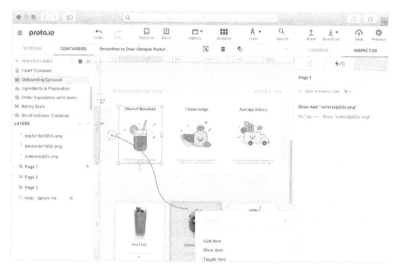

Proto.io enables you to create advanced prototypes with animations and transitions.

UXPin

UXPin is not only a wireframing tool but also a pretty advanced prototyping tool. You can also import designs from Sketch and Photoshop to see all the layers, then let the fun begin. UXPin comes with a tool to easily add basic interactions and create advanced animations.

Framer

Framer is for advanced users, since you have to know CoffeeScript to use it. You don't have to be a programmer to use it, but it takes time to learn. The possibilities are huge with Framer. For instance, you have access to the phone's camera. It comes with a simple design interface to help you make changes to designs easily, and it even allows you to build up the visual designs inside the tool.

Flinto for Mac

Flinto is a lightweight desktop tool for Mac. It's easy to get started and put together a simple mobile app. The focus is on the animation side and using gestures to control the prototype.

Type	What is it good for?	Tools
Wireframe prototype	Shows the basics of the product. Saves you time and money because the most important issues will surface at this stage. Use wireframe prototypes to usability test the product in the early stages.	Figma, UXPin, Axure RP, Marvel, Adobe XD, Justinmind, InVision
Design prototype	Lets you see and test out the final visual design of the product. Saves you time and money because plenty of issues can be resolved before implementing the designs.	Figma UXPin, Axure RP, Marvel, Adobe XD, Justinmind, InVision

Type	What is it good for?	Tools
High-fidelity prototype	Great to show how a single feature, animation, or transition should look. It's primarily for experimenting when the click-through prototypes aren't enough.	Framer, Principle, Flinto, Origami Studio

Go for a usability test with the visual designs.

Once you have the visual designs, it's essential to go out and usability test them. This is the moment when the users can see the final product design. Doing a usability test with the visual designs will show you how easy it is to use the product. What questions can be answered by usability testing the visual designs?

- Do people find the visual design attractive?
- What feelings and emotions does the design create inside the users?
- Does the visual design help users understand how the product works?
- Can users easily navigate their way through the product? Can they use each function with ease?
- Is the content clear and appealing? Is the microcopy well-worded and well-placed?

After the test, build in the feedback and make changes to the product. The goal is that users can perform all the crucial tasks inside the product with ease.

Key takeaways

- You don't have to be a visual designer to understand what makes a great design. In fact, everyone on the team can benefit by understanding these guidelines.
- Before diving into the visual design, make sure you set principles for the design first. Come up with five adjectives the designs should reflect. Use the spectrum of attributes to set expectations for the visuality. The goal during the design is to match these criteria.
- The first step in design is to create the "Look and Feel" designs. Create two to three different visual design concepts for a selected wireframe to experiment with different approaches.
- When you create the detailed visual design, pay attention to every detail. Design all states of the elements (empty, hover, disabled), create onboarding to help first-time users understand the product, and design notifications and error handling intuitively so users can recover from mistakes or errors.
- You have to know the difference between designing for the web and designing for mobile. Be aware of the touch-friendly zones of a device, and always preview every single design you create on a mobile device.
- During the Design phase, the content should be well-prepared. Use images with purpose and think of them as a type of content. Always pay attention to microcopy, as it takes minimal time to write but has a huge impact on the experience.
- Always create click-through prototypes from the visual designs and usability test them. This way, you'll save a huge amount of time and energy. You can avoid several flaws and resolve issues that otherwise would surface during the development.

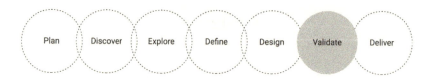

Plan   Discover   Explore   Define   Design   Validate   Deliver

#6 Validate

Test Out The Designs

The Validate phase is about testing out the designs and the product that you're building. If you want to build a good product (which you do), you have to validate the designs that you create. In this chapter, we're going to cover three ways to validate the designs:

1. Measuring the first impressions

First impressions count. It doesn't matter if it's a website or a mobile app, if users don't understand what the interfaces are about, they'll leave and try elsewhere. To understand what the impressions of the users are, we're going to apply five-second tests and click tests to fine tune the first experience of the users.

2. Evaluating the usability

I'm always using the terms "easy to use" and "convenient." I know you're sick of it. However, being straightforward and intuitive is the cornerstone of our work.

Usability tests will show you the issues and difficulties that users have while using your product. Based on this feedback, you can make changes to the product and build something valuable.

3. Validating designs with A/B testing

You might know a thing or two about A/B testing. It's the method used to determine whether a new version of a screen performs better than the old one. In this section, we're going to cover when and how to use A/B testing, how to make data-informed decisions, and what to do if you can't do A/B tests.

Measuring first impressions

When you enter a website, you spend around 10 to 15 seconds deciding whether to stay or leave the page. This is a frightening but fascinating statistic. It's frightening because it means you have just a fraction of time to convince the users to stay on your website. It's fascinating because the human mind can process a lot of information and make informed decisions quickly.

If you think about it, a few seconds isn't enough time to explore a website and read the text. Most decisions are made subconsciously. You have a concept in your mind about how things should work—how a website or product should look and behave. These concepts are called mental models, and they play an important role in product design. When something looks and works as expected, it matches your mental model. That's when you say, "This is intuitive!"

Take Tinder for instance. You have a mental model of somebody that you find attractive based on your past experiences and social and personal expectations. When you're swiping on Tinder and stop to say, "Oh! He's/she's gorgeous!" that person matches your mental model.

The same applies to when you're looking for information on the web or starting to use an app. You have a preconception of what you're looking for; that's why you know it when you find it. Mental models contain various information about a product or function. What does it look like? How do I use it? Well, look at the knob below. You know right away that you have to turn it to adjust the volume. This is a mental model that you learned in the physical world. If you had to push it or pull it, that would be surprising and misleading—something you didn't see coming.

Volume

You know how to use this knob because you have a mental model of it.

Earlier, we discussed how people tend to continue using a product in the first way that worked for them. They don't look for ways to improve the workflow or make it more efficient. You might be surprised, but a lot of users are still entering URLs into the Google search bar. Even stranger, many people enter "Google" into Bing or Yahoo, and the other way around.

This is because most people don't have a precise mental model of how browsers and search engines work.But, they get it done somehow. It works, so there's no need to think about it. You have to understand the mental models of your users. You have to understand what past experiences and prior knowledge they have and what they expect to see when they enter your website, download your app, or start to use your web application. Based on these first impressions, users will decide whether to stay or to abandon your product.

What makes users leave a product?

Below, you'll see five common deal breakers. Use this as a checklist, and go through your product to make sure you don't fall into any of these common pitfalls. Remember that there are still plenty of uncommon pitfalls that might come up later.

#1: Showing irrelevant content to users

Showing irrelevant content is usually a deal breaker. Imagine that you're searching for something in Google. You have a preconception of what you're looking for. When you see the results, you know you're on the right track. "Here we go, relevant results!" You select a page, but when it loads you feel scammed. If you don't find the site or information relevant, you'll go back to the search engine. Seventy-nine percent of people who don't like what they find on one site will go back and search for another site.

This all comes down to targeting. You have to make sure you drive the right visitors to the product and to the specific pages. You have to make sure that the content they see is relevant.

#2: Taking too long to show users what they're looking for

People don't spend much time looking for something on a website. They want it now. Remember, they usually spend between 10 to 15 seconds searching. If they don't find what they're looking for fast enough, they'll leave. This issue is related to the information architecture, which is, in essence, where you place each piece of information. A good information architecture will help the users find the information they're looking for. Prioritization is also crucial. You have to know what's important to the users and what's not. Showing them their priorities will make them engage with the product.

Another important thing you have to know is that people don't read a website—they scan it. This means that, instead of reading a website from beginning to end, we scan and scroll through the screen reading parts of the text. We do this to get a sense of what the page is about and what's relevant to us. The goal is to decide whether it's good enough to invest time into reading more. When scanning a screen, we look for the visually prominent elements—headlines, images, buttons, and lists. Likewise, we favor text that's easy and quick to read.

You have to design for scanning. Show only the necessary text, and break it down into chunks so it's easy to read. Use images and other visual elements to make the design simple and to hold the attention of the users.

#3 Using the wrong visual language

The human mind can process visual information 60,000 times as fast as legible text. This brings us to the fact that visuals have a huge influence on our decision to stay on or to leave a website. The visual design builds credibility and trust. You have to match the mental model of the users. They

262

expect a certain visuality based on their past experiences, impressions, and other sources of information.

I have a great example; I designed a payment page just for you. I'm sure you've seen a lot of payment pages. This is where you have to enter your credit card details to complete the checkout process. Since you have to enter sensitive information, the site has to build up trust; otherwise, you won't enter your credit card information. Take a look at this payment page:

"Superb design for a payment page," said no one ever.

I don't know if you can make it out, but those are actual ponies in the background. And for all you designers, yes, it is Comic Sans. What happened here? You had a mental model of a payment page—clean, sophisticated, trustworthy, and so on. When you saw this screen, it was a mismatch with your mental model. As a result, you probably felt uncomfortable about the page and would not have entered your credit card details.

Good visual language

- builds trust in the users,
- helps the users better navigate inside the product,
- helps users understand the information architecture, and
- creates an appealing and desirable image of the product in the user's head.

A bad visual design

- destroys trust and credibility,
- makes the product less accessible, and
- frustrates the user.

#4 Using improper communication

Just as in real life, you have to know how to communicate with different people; the same rules apply to the digital world.

- Common problems with communication:
- Using the wrong tone—not using the correct tone for a particular audience is a mistake.
- Using too much text or text that's too difficult to understand—a common mistake is the use of jargon that users don't understand.
- Using impersonal communication—people don't like it when they feel the content is for just anybody; it has to be personal and target the potential users.
- Bombarding visitors with ads—don't get me wrong; ads have their place in marketing and business. But when ads make it difficult to perform a task or consume content, they can backfire and create a bad impression on the users. You have to find a balance. Bombard-

ing users with ads will decrease their engagement. However, the more time they spend in the product, the more chances you have to show ads.

- Poor grammar and spelling mistakes—these issues make your product feel amateur and messy. The point is, would you buy something from somebody who doesn't care enough to write proper sentences?
- Poor content—having bad content (like articles or videos) is worse than having no content. Bad content will destroy your brand. This includes having bad quality or irrelevant photos. Images are also part of communication. If they're of poor quality or too artificial, (like every stock photo on Earth) users will find them impersonal and fake.

Testing first impressions with five-second tests

Since users make up their minds very quickly, we need a test that's very fast. During a five-second test, we show an image to the users (e.g., a screenshot of a website) for exactly five seconds. Then, the image disappears, and we ask a couple of questions. Five seconds is not enough time to deeply explore the image. It's only enough time to get a rough idea. After looking at a webpage for five seconds, you'll only remember the most prominent elements, a few words, and how it made you feel. This is the exact information we're looking for.

Questions that can be answered with a five-second test:

- Can users recall crucial elements on a page (e.g., call-to-action buttons or other elements that we want them to find quickly)?

- Do users know what the brand is about?
- Do users know what the product or service is about?
- What and who do users think the product is for?
- What words do users use to describe the brand/product?
- Do users know what the design is about?
- Do users know how to use the product?
- Do users like the design?
- Do users find the product trustworthy?

You can do five-second tests with a lot of different products and designs. Here's what you can test out:

- Screenshots of a website or web application
- Screens of a mobile application
- Logos and brand identities
- Print materials (brochures, flyers, etc.)
- Physical products (wearables, packaging design, etc.)

As for the designs, you can test both wireframes and visual designs. Testing wireframes will show you if the users understand the structure of the site, the wording, and what the screen is about. Testing the visual design will show you if the users like the design, what elements they can recall, and what their overall impression was.

You can do a five-second test anywhere in the process. It's done quickly (with a recruitment service, it only takes a couple of hours to complete). If you're not sure about how to build up a screen, do a quick test to see if users get the idea or not. If you're about to redesign a page, it's worthwhile to do a quick test to see what users think about the current design. Five-second tests can be done in person or remotely. Doing it in person means you sit down with potential users and show them the designs for five seconds, then you ask some questions. It's doable this way; however, I advise doing it remotely. Multiple platforms like UsabilityHub and Optimal Workshop offer five-second testing (along with other testing methods).

Do a five-second test!

Choose which design to test.

The first step is to choose which design to test. You can use analytics to identify which screens to test out. It's worthwhile to test pages with lots of traffic or high bounce rates. You can also test the most important pages (e.g., the main page, sign-up flow, and pricing page). What are the most critical pages? Which screen do you have to get right in order to not lose visitors? You can also use five-second tests to see what people think about your logo, brand, or packaging design.

Create the image and upload it to UsabilityHub.

I recommend starting with UsabilityHub. It's easy and free to get started and offers a recruitment service to invite test participants. You can even specify demographics. Simply create the screenshots or images you want to test and upload them to UsabilityHub. If you want to test multiple designs at the same time, create separate tests.

Come up with questions.

Asking the right questions is what this test is all about. You can stick with the three questions we discussed in the Explore chapter:

- Do they know what the page/logo/brand is about?
- Do they know what to do on that screen?
- Do they know how to navigate it?

Moreover, you can ask them about their impressions. What words would they use to describe the design? Do they find it trustworthy? Do they like the logo or design? If you're designing a landing page, it's crucial that users understand what the site is about in under five seconds. This is why you can ask these questions, but don't expect them to remember what was in the upper right corner. As a rule of thumb, don't ask for small details. And whatever you do, don't ask them to recall text.

Invite test participants and start the test.

All the tools will create a unique link that you can send to potential users. They open the link, find the instructions, and take the test. If you do the test on UsabilityHub, you can choose to use their recruitment service. This means that you specify who you want to test (gender, location, level of education, and age), and they send the test out to high-quality test participants. All you have to do is sit back and wait for the responses (which usually take a couple of hours to deliver).

The downside of this method is that it's a paid service, and it's not as well-targeted as testing with your real users. Having said that, it's worthwhile to build a database of potential users who are willing to take your tests. For a five-second test, you want to have 20 to 50 responses. The margin of error is less than 15% with more than 40 participants.

Analyze results and make changes to the product.

UsabilityHub will generate a word cloud from the responses as well as show the full responses. When analyzing the results, look for how many correct and incorrect answers you have. You'll see what people can make out from your designs.

Based on this feedback, make changes to the product and test again! Likewise, you can test multiple variations at the same time. The goal is to make sure the most important parts of the product are clear and people can understand them quickly.

Click tests: Test if your users know where to click

Usability tests play an important role in UX. These tests can show what works well in the product and what should be improved. Click tests are like micro-usability tests. We can only ask one question, and the users can only perform one task at a time. During a click test, we show a design to the users and give them a task to perform. The goal is to learn where the users would click on the designs to perform a certain task. As with usability tests, we use scenarios. Scenarios are little stories that put users into context. Let's say you have an e-commerce site that sells shoes (by the way, THIS IS a scenario). You want to know if users can easily find where to click to select a shoe size. In this case, your scenario would be,

"Imagine you're shopping for shoes. You already chose a pair that you like and are about to select a size. Where would you click to select a size for the shoes?"

The goal of click testing is to find out if the users can identify the key interactions on a screen. Do they know where to click? According to statistics, users who choose the right path the first time are 87% more likely to succeed. On the other hand, users who take the wrong path at first only have a 46% success rate.

When analyzing the results of a click test, consider the following:

1. Accuracy of clicks

Accuracy is a measure of how many people clicked on the right place compared how many people clicked elsewhere. A percentage can be calculated based on this data. The higher the percentage you have, the better. I recommend aiming for greater than 90% accuracy.

2. How much time it takes to do the tests

Time is a crucial factor in these tests. Believe it or not, people aren't stupid. If you give them a task, in time they'll figure out how to solve it. But remember, our goal is to make it as quickly solvable as possible because in real life users won't spend time figuring out how to use something if they don't get it right away. If the average time for completion is between 0 and 10 seconds, you can be happy. You did a great job, and it's clear to everyone. Buy yourself a donut.

If it's between 10 and 20 seconds, that's not so good. Think about it! If your job is to locate a button (after reading the instructions, which is not counted in the time) and click on it, 20 seconds is an insanely long time. You have to improve this. Think about how to simplify the task and make it more intuitive for your users. If it's more than 30 seconds... Come on! The grass grows faster than that!

Aside from these two factors, after the test, you can ask users how they felt about it. How confident did they feel during the test? How difficult was the task for them? This will help you get a better understanding of how your users think.

Click-sequence test

You can add more screens in a test and link them together (like in InVision). This is called a click-sequence test. This way, you can show a flow to the users (e.g., a checkout flow). The users can select an item, put it in the cart, proceed to checkout, and hit pay. In this test, we have to examine each step individually (accuracy, time, and confidence level). Use click-sequence tests to test out navigation and multi-step processes in your product.

Do a click test!

Decide which interaction or task to test.
The first thing to do is to choose what you want to test. An easy way is to start by testing the CTA buttons. Identify what your users have to do on each screen, and look for complex solutions or solutions that aren't straightforward.

Create the images and upload them to UsabilityHub.
After you've uploaded the images, you have to tell the software where people should click. It's just like creating hotspots in InVision. You can also specify how many times the users can click on a screen.

Write the scenario.
Write a short and informative scenario. Tell the users how they arrived at the screen and what they should do there. Then, add a specific task to perform (Show me how you would do x, or Where you would click to do x). Be short and helpful.

Send it to the users.
Just like the five-second tests, you can either use the UsabilityHub recruit-

ment service, or you can send the test to a list of potential users using the link generated by the tool. Aim for 20 to 50 responses for this test.

Run the test and analyze results.

UsabilityHub will present the results in a heatmap format. You'll see where the users clicked. The more users clicked on the spot, the "hotter" it will appear. Start by analyzing the ratio of good to bad clicks. You can even segment the clicks and analyze different user groups. Remember to pay attention to the time as well!

Next, look at the bad clicks. What could have gone wrong? Maybe there's something confusing in the design. Maybe users tried to click on something that wasn't clickable. Interestingly, this last one happens quite often. If you see people clicking on something that's not clickable, think about it. Why did they click there? What did they expect to see?

Refine and test again.

Based on the feedback, make changes to the product, then test again. The point is to make sure that the most important interactions are clear right away.

Evaluating the usability

Usability testing is the Swiss Army knife of UX. Usability shows you how easy and convenient it is to use a product. Some people confuse usability with user experience, but that's a huge mistake. User experience includes usability (think of the staircase of UX), but it goes beyond that.

During a usability test, we ask the test participants to look at our product and perform a few given tasks. While doing so, we—as the test facilitators—listen and take notes. We don't tell users how to use the product; we just let them try it out. This is harder than it sounds, but this is the way to do it.

The goal is to understand the weaknesses of the product. We want to see where users get lost in the process and where they seem confused or frustrated. We collect practical feedback on what should be improved in order to make the product more user-friendly.

How users should use your product, and how they actually do use it. Users often take a different approach.

During a usability test, we

- see if users can perform tasks with the product and how much time the tasks take,
- uncover the usability issues of the product,
- see what's clear and what's confusing to the users,
- understand how appealing the design is and how satisfied the users are with the product, and
- uncover issues that otherwise would only surface after the development.

However, you have to know the limits of usability testing. One of the most common fails in UX is using usability testing to validate whether people would buy the product. While you might collect some feedback on the product idea during a usability test, it won't be significant. It's also important to keep the focus of the test. Remember, it's purpose is to understand whether what we designed actually works. That's all.

Who to invite for a usability test

Most of the time, we have to recruit potential users for the tests. This is the best way to get meaningful feedback. The more feedback you have from potential buyers, the more likely it is that you're going in the right direction with the product. It also depends on who the product or feature is for. For example, if you're designing an onboarding process for first-time users, it makes no sense to do tests with existing users. However, if you're working on something for returning or power users, you have to recruit your existing users—which is slightly easier. The rule of thumb for usability tests is to give it to people who have never used or seen the interface before.

How many participants do I need?

It's best to have five participants for a usability test. This might seem like a small number but, remember, this is a qualitative test. We're after the "whys." Eighty-five percent of usability issues surface after testing with three to six participants. Above five to six users, you're going to see the same problems and issues again and again. This is because the second user will perform the same tasks as the first one, so there'll be an overlap between the two tests. People are different, so there'll be some more issues on the second and third tests, but you'll mostly see the same things. This is why, with more than five participants, you'll get less and less helpful information. Instead, do a round of usability tests with five users, then make changes to the product and test again. This way, you can test out the changes and keep improving the product step by step.

Doing a usability test on a current product

When you already have a product and want to improve it, it's often best to start with a usability test so you can see what should be improved first. This is true for doing a complete redesign of a website or a web app and when you just want to improve a certain part or function in the product. Doing a usability test on a current product will show you the weaknesses of the product.

As a result, you'll have a prioritized list of things you have to change. I also recommend doing a usability test when there are so many things to improve that you're not sure where to start. In this case, a usability test will help you prioritize and focus on the weakest parts of the product.

Doing a usability test on the competitor's product

You can learn a lot from the competitors by doing a usability test on their product. This will show you how users use a similar product. What are the strengths—that you can keep—and the weaknesses—that you should avoid—of the product? The biggest benefit is getting ideas for new features and products. Ask the users to show you how they use the competitor's product and look for ways to improve on it.

Usability testing the wireframes

We covered this test type in the Define chapter. Usability testing the wireframe prototypes is one of the most important tests you can run. Wireframes are flexible and easy to modify, and they show you how the product will look and behave. Doing a usability test on the wireframes will show you what you should improve before going into visual design. This will save you a lot of time because it's easier to iterate the wireframes than to iterate the visual designs.

Usability testing the visual design

As we discussed in the Design chapter, you should do a usability test when you have the final visual designs. The same applies with wireframes. It's easier to make changes to the visual design and resolve usability issues here than in the final working product. Just remember that 85% of usability issues can be learned by doing a test with five users. If you fail to test out the designs, you'll have to start making changes to the working product after months of development. Doing a usability test on the visual designs will show you how easy it is to use the product and will enable you to resolve a lot of issues to fine tune the experience. Relax, you'll still have enough work to do when your product goes live.

Usability testing the working product

Usability testing is not just for prototypes. You can do a test with real working products. In fact, usability testing the current product means testing the working product. In the live product, everything works (hopefully). You have all the functions, so it's the final form of the experience. That's why it's crucial to test them out. Still not convinced? Well, I'll tell

276

you one thing that you'll never experience while testing prototypes—bugs in the working product. Doing a usability test with the working product will help you test and refine the animations, transitions, and interactive elements of the product and eliminate bugs.

Remote test versus in-person test

I recommend doing the tests in person. By the way, it's easier to recruit users for a usability test than for an interview. Doing the tests in person will give you more detailed feedback from the users. You'll see how they react and what gestures they use, hear how they talk, and witness all the little things and impressions that can be valuable when it comes to empathizing with them. But, if you can't do the tests in person, you can do them remotely.

Remote tests have some inherent advantages. They're quicker to set up, so you can do more tests in less time. Remote tests are a good solution when you're targeting users that are difficult to reach or too busy to come to your tests.

You can do a remote test in two ways: moderated (using a screen sharing tool) or unmoderated (using a platform to conduct the test).

Moderated remote usability testing

Moderated means that you control the events of the test. You use a screen sharing tool (e.g., Skype or Zoom) to see the user's screen. This is very similar to an in-person test, but you don't have to be in the same place as the user. There are multiple tools that can help you conduct tests in this manner. For example, InVision has a function called LiveShare. It allows you to co-browse the designs—you can see where the users click and what they do with the designs. There are also co-browsing tools like Surfly that let you browse a website or web app together with the users and see the same screen.

The advantage of this method is that you don't have to be in the same location (or time zone) as the users. It's also easier to set up. So, whenever you can't perform in-person tests, go for moderated remote tests.

Unmoderated remote usability testing

Unmoderated means that you don't have control over the tests; you upload the designs or provide a link to the users along with the tasks and questions they have to answer, and the users do the rest. There are several companies that provide unmoderated usability tests. Most of them offer ways to recruit test participants as well. All you have to do is upload the designs, tell them whom you want to test (e.g., specify demographics), write the task, and sit back and wait for the videos.

The upside is that it takes minimal time to run. You need the designs and the test instructions, but that's it. You don't have to worry about recruiting or conducting the tests; you just sit back and analyze the results. The downside is that you can't guide the users, and you don't see their reactions and expressions. When you see something interesting, you can't modify your questions. You can only analyze the data you have. Therefore, only use unmoderated tests when there's no time or no budget for moderated tests.

Testing on mobile devices

Mobile testing isn't another sort of usability test; it's just testing designs of mobile apps or mobile versions of websites. However, it's vital that I remind you that you must only test mobile designs on mobile devices. This is the only way to get meaningful feedback, because this is the only way users will have access to the product.

Recording the test is a bit more tricky. You can use an application like UX Recorder or Lookback to record the device screens. The simplest solution is to use another phone or camera to record the test on video. The advantage of this solution is that you can also see how the users hold the phone and how they move their fingers.

Do a usability test!

Select the type of test.

First, decide what you want to test and how you want to conduct the test. The "what" can be a prototype, a working version of the product, the full product, or parts of it. The "how" can be in person, remote, or unmoderated.

Invite users.

Next, recruit five participants. Recruiting can take some time, so I recommend starting early. The best time to start is two weeks or more before the test. You can find a detailed guide to recruiting in the Discover chapter.

Write tasks and scenarios.

During a usability test, you can ask the users to do three things:

- Perform a specific task.
- Discover the product.
- Answer open-ended questions.

Tasks and scenarios

When preparing a usability test, you have to list the things users can do inside the product (e.g., buy a product, use the search engine, or subscribe to download an e-book). The goal is to test out these interactions. Most of these interactions take multiple steps. For example, buying milk on an e-commerce site would consist of the following:

- Browse the products and select the milk.
- Specify the quantity.
- Add it to the shopping cart.
- Open the cart/proceed to checkout.
- Enter your personal details (shipping, billing info, etc.).
- Select the payment method.
- Review the order.
- Pay (via a payment page or 3rd party interface like PayPal).
- Determine success or failure.

These are the steps the user must take, and this is what you want to evaluate. How much time did they spend on each task? Is there room for improvement? How could you deliver a better experience?

But, you can't give these tasks directly to the users because you have to see if they can find their way through the product first. This is when scenarios come into the picture. A scenario is a short story that we tell the users to get a better understanding of who they are, why they use the product, and what they want to do with the product. A good scenario will help the users imagine a situation in which they would use the product.

EXAMPLE:

You're going to test an e-commerce site to see if people can easily buy milk. You give a scenario like this:

"Imagine that you run out of milk at home. It's late, and the grocery store is closed. A friend recommended an online grocery shopping site with fast next day delivery. You go to their site, and this is how you end up seeing the following screen. Show me how you would order three gallons of milk with express next day delivery. Don't forget to narrate your thoughts aloud."

Product discovery

For product discovery, simply ask users to start using the product as they normally would, and ask them to narrate their thoughts. We're interested in how they interpret the designs. Can they identify the screens? Do they know how to start? Do they know what each function is used for? Do they understand the elements on a screen?

<u>Think-aloud protocol</u>

Ask the participants to explicitly speak every thought and impression they have out loud during the test—what they see, where they are, what they're doing, and why they're doing it. This is called the think-aloud protocol, and it's a cornerstone of usability tests. You want to hear things like this:

"I click on read more to see more information on this product. Okay, now this confuses me. I expected to see a new page, but I don't know what this is. Ah, okay, so I have to scroll down to see the rest of the information."

Open-ended questions

It's worthwhile to ask open-ended questions at the end of the test. For example:

- How did you feel during the test?
- What were your impressions about the visual design?
- What did you like about the product?
- What did you dislike about the product?

- What caused you frustration or made you feel disappointed?
- How would you rate the experience of the product on a scale from one to ten, with one being awful and ten being superb?

Prepare the test.

To run the test, make sure you've prepared everything:

- Peaceful environment (desk, chair, and nobody trolling in the background)
- Laptop/mobile phone with reliable internet connection
- Screen recorder or camera
- Printed consent forms
- Printed login credentials and other technical details

The last two things are interesting. You need to record the screens, both video and audio. Make sure you clearly ask the participants to agree to be recorded. Ask them to sign the consent form so the agreement is documented.

Also, prepare information like login credentials if necessary. If you're testing a web app, don't waste time finding your login email and password. Create a demo account (or let the users create one) and provide the password for it. If the users have to enter specific information (e.g., sign up), have a sheet of paper with the necessary information printed on it.

Software

Always record the user screens during the test. This enables you to rewatch the session later to focus on the details. You'll also be able to focus on the user (their emotions and gestures) and not have to jot down everything you observe right at that moment. There are a couple of dedicated tools on the market. Lookback, for example, lets you test on any device and any platform (mobile, desktop, MacOS, Windows, iOS, and

Android). When you're done with the test, you simply hit stop. The program will automatically upload it to the cloud where you can see it, comment on it, and share it. Lookback is a professional choice for people who often conduct usability tests.

Do a pilot test!

It's worthwhile to do a pilot test first. Even though I'm a seasoned tester, I still prefer starting with a pilot test. Have a colleague or friend act as a user and do the whole scene. Make sure the prototype works and the recording environment is set up correctly so the test will run smoothly.

Do I have to pay the users?

In my experience, it's best not to pay test participants. Here's why: If you're solving a real problem, there will be users who are experiencing that problem. Most of the time, people like to talk about the problems they have, and they're interested in talking to people who are trying to solve those problems. As a matter of fact, you can even use this as a micro-validation of the problem—if you can easily get five people to test your designs just because they're interested, chances are, you're on the right track.

However, giving a gift to the participants is good practice; it can be a gift card or something related to the company. Users will be surprised and happy to receive it, which boosts their engagement.

If you can't recruit users, or it takes too much time to recruit them, you can offer a gift card or another form of incentive in return for their time. In this case, make sure you explicitly ask them to be honest. You want to hear their honest feedback regardless of the fact they're being paid. Explain to them that it's vital not to be biased during the test.

Invite team members to the test.

It's good practice to invite clients, stakeholders, and team members to the test. This is so they'll be able to see what the actual users are doing with the product. It's great to show designers how users are using the product they designed. Developers and stakeholders can learn about the real-life users and their behaviors. Be cautious though. You don't want your users to feel like they're in a petting zoo. Remember that you have to create a relaxed and comfortable environment. If you have a lab room with a separate room for inspection, use that. If you don't, there are pieces of software that will let you mirror the screen of a device so people in the next room can view it without disturbing the participant. Try the Reflektor app, for instance, which mirrors and streams the device's screen wirelessly.

Run the usability test.

Before doing the test, run through your checklist:

- Tools are prepped, and batteries are fully charged.
- Screen recording is ready.
- Mobile phones are charged and muted.
- Snacks and drinks are prepared.
- Handouts and consent forms are ready.

When the users arrive, greet them casually and give them time to warm up with five to ten minutes of chit-chat. Make sure they feel relaxed and comfortable. Then, explain to them how the test works. Ask for their permission to record their screen and voice. Tell them how important their feedback is, and thank them for dedicating their time to the test.

Set the rules for the test:

- The users cannot make mistakes. Any issues come down to you and the product. Tell them not to stress if they don't understand something. You're not testing them; you're testing the product.

Tell them that when they don't understand something or don't know how to use something to simply move along.

- Reinforce the think-aloud protocol. Ask them to narrate all of their thoughts—what they're thinking, what they're doing, and why they're doing it. Sometimes you have to tell them this a few times to get them talking.
- Tell them that you're there to listen and observe and that you won't stop them if they make a mistake or need help.
- Thank them again for participating. Remind them that their feedback is of great value to the product!

Instructions for testers:

- Get the users to talk! This is vital. Tell them to narrate their thoughts. If they're not narrating their thoughts, tell them again and again until they start doing it.
- Don't stop the user, don't tell them what they should do, and don't give instructions. Most importantly, don't grab the mouse and show them what to do. This may seem obvious, but you'd be surprised.
- If they ask you questions like, "What does this button do?" or "What should I do here?" Don't answer the questions. Instead, ask them to tell you what they're thinking and to do what they think they should do.
- Always leave time for the users to think and complete the tasks. Don't rush and push them to speed up if they're slow or hesitant.
- If they get stuck and ask for help, tell them everything's okay and that they didn't do anything wrong. Make a note, and move them forward in the process.
- During the test, don't tell them anything about the product. Focus on the scenario instead. If the user is interested (which is a good sign), you can discuss the product when the test is over.

Take notes!

The test is recorded so we can re-watch it later, but it's still crucial to write down your thoughts and observations during the test. These notes will serve as a guide when you're analyzing the results. Make a note when the user makes a mistake, gets lost, or seems frustrated. Make a note if something surprises you! It's worth taking notes of good things as well. It's also a great practice to invite a team member to take the notes for you while you facilitate the test.

Closing

When the users are done with the tasks, ask a few follow-up questions (the open-ended questions discussed earlier). Ask them about how they felt, how they liked the product, or what they would improve. You can also talk about the product itself. Remember, you have to build a participant database, so don't forget to ask them if they would be willing to come again. Then, thank them for their time and start the next session.

Analyze the results.

The main goal of the analysis is to gather the findings of the test and document them in a way that's feasible for the team. To put it simply, if the results are actionable, you can use them to create a better design. If they're not, they'll end up in your mailbox in the form of a fancy PDF that no one cares about.

When you're done with all the tests, do three things:

- Evaluate the tasks.
- Create a backlog of the issues.
- Write the usability report.

Task evaluation

Before coming up with the scenarios, we created a list of tasks users have to perform inside the product. The first analysis technique is to evaluate these tasks. To do the analysis, you'll need the video recordings of the tests and your notes.

Go through each task and ask yourself the following questions:

- Did the users solve the task successfully? How many users solved the task?
- How much time did they spend on the task?
- How confident were they while completing the task?

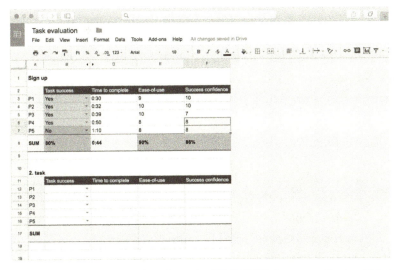

The Task Evaluation template from the 7STEPUX® Resource Center. This is an easy way to see which tasks have to be improved.

The easiest way to document the task evaluation is to create a spreadsheet where you can keep track of all this information. All you have to do is upload every task, specify which participants were successful, and specify which of them failed. Then, add how much time each user spent on completing the task. Finally, rate how confident they were while solving the task using a scale of 1 to 10—with 10 being laser-focused, and 1 being like playing Marco Polo.

Create a backlog of the usability issues.
You'll notice a lot of issues during the test, and you'll get feedback from the users. We need a practical way to document this information. I'm going to show you two methods for this. The simplest way is to create a Trello board.

METHOD 1: Use Trello
Trello is a free tool used to organize information. It's very flexible and can be used to keep track of to-dos or as a project management tool. Creating a backlog of usability issues in Trello is the easiest way to have actionable output for the test. Start by dedicating a board to the test. Then, create lists for pages, tasks, and scenarios—whatever works for you. The idea is that you need a way to group the feedback.

After this, you can start adding cards. Each card should include

- a usability issue (e.g., "didn't find the checkout button" or "not sure how to use x"),
- a remark from the tester (e.g., "xyz isn't working" or "there's no success message at x"), and
- feedback or an idea from the user (e.g., "would be happy to have an x feature").

It's pretty simple, right? You can also use Trello's further functionality to enhance your backlog.

- Use [ ] to identify the different types of feedback, such as [issue], [remark], [idea].

- Create labels to indicate priority. Use red for high-priority or severe issues, orange for medium-priority, and yellow or blue for low-priority.
- You can invite team members and assign them to certain tasks. This comes in handy since there will be different kinds of feedback. There will be feedback for the developers (fix bugs), feedback for the designers (come up with a better design), and feedback for the product, which is relevant to the product manager (new feature ideas).

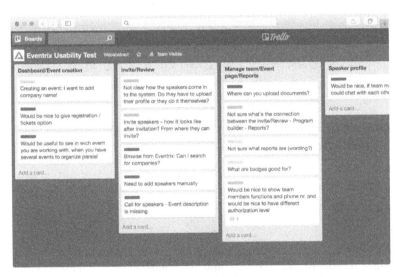

Create a Trello board to keep track of usability issues and ideas that come up during a usability test.

METHOD 2: Use the Issue Backlog spreadsheet

You can also use a spreadsheet for the analysis. If you use a spreadsheet, you can enter more data without becoming too overwhelmed and losing track of information. The template we use includes how many users experienced a certain issue.

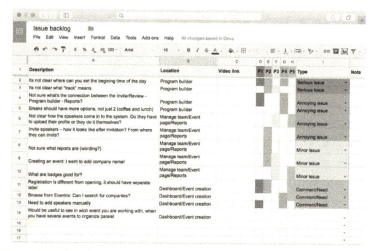

The Issue Backlog spreadsheet makes it easy for you to keep track of all the information and feedback you obtain during the test. By using rainbow columns, you can see the patterns that emerge between participants.

Description

Describe the issue or feedback in one sentence.

Example: "User didn't find the 'add to cart' button." Or, "User wasn't sure how to select a size."

Location

Where did the problem occur (on which page or screen)? This will make it easier for you and the team to locate the issue.

Example: "cart page" or "home page"

Link to the video

Linking to the video will enable others to see what the user did. This is also extremely helpful for you when you have to present the findings of the tests to stakeholders.

P1 – P5

P1 – P5 stands for the participants. Each participant is indicated with a different color; that's why it's also called a rainbow spreadsheet. You can indicate with color that a problem occurred when using a large sample size.

Use this for prioritization. The more participants experience an issue or give feedback on it, the more important it is.

Evaluation

Based on the feedback, you have to evaluate each issue:

- **Serious issue**
  A serious issue prevents the users from doing something and stops them in the process.
- **Annoying issue**
  An annoying issue means that users were able to complete the task, but with difficulty.
- **Minor issue**
  A minor issue is one that doesn't really disturb or annoy the users. You can enhance the product and fine tune the experience by resolving these issues.
- **Comment/Need**
  There will be feedback that isn't about an issue or problem. This can be a user/tester comment or a request for a feature.

Write the usability report!

It's good practice to write a short summary of the test. Don't spend too much time and energy on it—just sum up the most important findings:

- What is the product (brief description)?
- Who are the target users?
- What is the test process (to present to stakeholders or top management)?
  - Explain how the usability test works.
  - Discuss the participants (how many were there, how were they recruited, etc.).
  - Discuss the tasks and scenarios.
- Present test findings:
  - Task evaluation
  - Problem backlog
- Recommendations and conclusion/next steps

Make changes to the product.

Once you have the analysis, you can move on and iterate the product. First, you have to discuss the findings of the test with the product team. The goal is to decide what feedback to implement and how to implement it.

The best way to do this is with a workshop. The facilitator of the test should present the findings and guide the team through the issue backlog. Discuss the feedback piece by piece and decide what the priorities are and how to move forward.

Prioritization

Since you'll have a lot of feedback, you have to prioritize wisely. You have to focus on the issues and feedback that you'll get the most benefit from. To do this, simply use the Implementation Priority Matrix.

Go through each issue and comment, and ask:

- How much impact do they have on the experience?
- How much time and energy is needed to implement them?

You'll end up with four buckets:

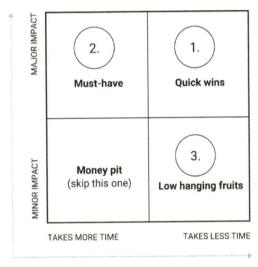

The Implementation Priority Matrix will help you keep your focus on the important things for the users and the business.

Quick-wins

The issues and comments that go into this bucket are easy to implement, and they have a huge impact on the user experience, so these are the first issues to address. Interestingly, most of the serious issues are in this bucket (e.g., confusing microcopy, unclear instructions, or simply a bad choice of colors). These things can cause frustration, so they really affect the experience. But, they're easy to resolve once you've identified them.

Must-have

The must-have bucket is full of ideas and changes that are necessary for the product. The issues in this bucket might take more time to implement, but they have a big impact on user experience. An example is when you have to redesign a flow or screen or you realize that there's a function that's not working as it should.

Low hanging fruit

If you see something that could improve the experience a bit and doesn't take too much time to address, it belongs in the low hanging fruit bucket. This bucket is full of small improvements and enhancements to the interface. These are great, but they only rank third in priority.

Money pit

If something doesn't have a real impact on user experience but requires a lot of effort to implement, you know you've run into a money pit. It's not always easy to spot money pits. A money pit can be a feature idea that seems great, but users want something different. Priorities are the things that help achieve the business goals and serve the user needs. I've seen people get excited by new feature ideas (after a usability test) that would only affect a small percentage of users. Moreover, they were just "nice to have" features that could, at best, enhance the user experience.

Why don't we start with the must-have bucket? You can start with the must-have bucket; however, in my experience, it's better to start with the quick wins. That way you can quickly achieve success and bring results to the team while giving you more time to work on the must-have bucket.

Finally, remember: test again; test often. Don't just do one test. Instead, form a habit. Use tests as milestones for the design and development of the product. Design, test, make changes to the product, and test again. That's the mantra of a great product team.

See? I told you there was more to come.

Validating designs with A/B testing

During an A/B test (also called a split test or multivariate test), you test out two different versions of a design and see which of them performs better. The difference between the versions can be small (like a button or color) or huge (like testing two different designs against each other).

The good thing about A/B testing is that it's really simple. You take a design (say a landing page) and make some changes to it (create a variation). Then use a tool which will show the users either the original version or the variation. Our job is to tell the tool what we consider success, or to put it another way, what the users should do in the designs and what the call-to-actions are. A call-to-action can be clicking on a button, the average time spent on the page, etc.

The tool then shows us which design performed better, the original or the variation. Take the winner and implement it in your product. Piece of cake, right?

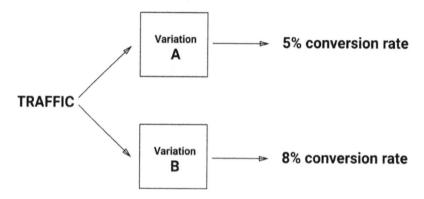

The logic of an A/B test. Split the traffic, show different versions to the visitors, and compare performance.

The downside of A/B tests is that they don't tell you why a variation performed better. They're just a measurement technique that you can use to test out the designs. To understand why a variation works better, and what the users think and feel, you need to apply qualitative research like interviews and usability tests. Think of A/B tests as a 0 or 1 machine. You put in the designs, and it will give you back a 0 or 1. Is the new version better or not?

It's very easy to put together an A/B test, but most people do it incorrectly. They think it's all about changing the color of a button and seeing the results. The truth is, they won't. The truth is that most A/B tests fail. So, before we get started, I'm going to walk you through how Not to do an A/B test!

Don't just test small changes (like colors)!

Most people think A/B tests are for making incremental changes to the product, such as testing out the color of a button. I feel bad about this because I started out with that example here since it's the easiest way to explain it. There are a few success stories on the internet about how Google tested 41 shades of blue and found the perfect one with A/B testing or how someone improved their conversions by changing the button color to orange, but these are exceptions. These stories are so persuasive that they impact A/B testing in a negative way.

The truth is, most of the time, testing colors is a waste of time. A color test is only good for one thing—to disappoint you and make you abandon A/B testing.

The solution

Don't push pixels and test button colors. You have to have a ton of traffic to get significant results or to see any results at all. Just think about it! If the information architecture of your landing page sucks, do you think it would make any difference if you had the right color for a button? Instead, focus on the information architecture, the copy, and the microcopy. Test the things that could have a great impact on the experience first.

Don't give up after the first fail!

Do you want to see the biggest roller coaster drop ever? Just look at the number of people who abandon A/B testing after the first fail. Most people test stupid things. They read about orange being the highest converting button color, and they go for it. They do a test, and it doesn't result in a significant change. It's tempting at this point to say that A/B testing is bullshit and walk away.

You have to accept that most of the tests won't bring results. In most companies one out of eight tests is successful. Most of the tests aren't significant or the variation doesn't beat the original. But that's okay.

The solution

Don't give up after the first unsuccessful test! Don't give up after the second one either! It takes time and practice to do good A/B tests. Even professionals have more unsuccessful tests than successful ones. Do yourself a favor—don't expect great results at first. That way, you'll save yourself from being disappointed.

Don't stop the test too early!

If you want to run an A/B test, you have to do the math first and calculate how big of a sample size you need to use and how long to run the test for it to be significant. It's simple math. However, a lot of people stop their tests too early. They don't pay attention to the sample size, or maybe they don't even know when the test is significant and when it's not.

A/B testing is a measurement technique. The point is to use data to make a better product. If you take data out of the picture, there's no point in testing. Without data you should just implement the changes. You still have a 50% chance of hitting the nail on the head.

The solution

Always calculate the sample size and time required for the test to be significant. When I say "significant," I mean that there's a 95% chance that a variation is performing better. Obviously, you can aim for a higher confidence level, but that will require more time and/or traffic.

Don't A/B test if you don't have enough traffic.

This is the downside to A/B tests. You need traffic. You need a decent amount of traffic. If you only have a couple hundred visitors a day, don't run A/B tests because they will probably take too long to be significant. You don't have the next thousand years to wait for the results.

This is simple math. There are several calculators on the internet that tell you how much traffic you need to run your tests. They'll also tell you how long you should run the tests in order for them to be significant. If it's going to take months, find a better tool.

The solution
Do the math and find out how much traffic you need. If you don't have enough, look for other solutions.

Do a usability test
Usability tests will show you the strengths and weaknesses of the product. Do a usability test, make changes to the product, and do the test again. This way, you'll measure the results in the real working product.

Do click tests and five-second tests
Click tests and five-second tests are good alternatives to A/B tests. They're extremely useful for testing out websites and landing pages, and you can use them to simulate A/B tests. Just create multiple versions of a landing page and run separate tests. The logic is the same as with A/B tests, but you can see results in hours rather than months.

Use analytics and visual analytics
First, use analytics to identify where users get lost and where they abandon the site (look for high bounce rates). Then, use a visual analytics tool to understand what could go wrong. Heatmaps—and especially video

session recordings—can go a long way to help you understand a usability issue. They allow you to work with real data. Once you've done this, you can make changes to the product and measure the performance of the new version.

Don't focus solely on A/B tests.

When it comes to testing, most people only think of A/B tests. They think, "We have to measure everything and make our decisions based on data." This is, and it's a good way to think about building products, but remember that A/B tests and data won't answer the "whys." They won't tell you anything about the needs, goals, and frustrations of your users. If you only do A/B tests, you're basing your decisions on guesses about what to improve.

Doing only A/B tests is guesswork.

The solution
Use research methods like user interviews and observation to understand what users think and feel. Use other test types like usability tests to un-

300

cover the usability issues of the product. Based on this feedback, identify what should be improved in the product. Then, make changes and run the A/B test.

What do you need to A/B test?

There are lots of articles and case studies on how to do A/B tests that bring results. Don't get me wrong; they're good and worth reading. But take my advice—only use them as a springboard. You have to focus on finding the problems in your product, not going through a checklist. According to statistics, most businesses that focus on identifying and resolving issues within their product are 74% more likely to reach success with A/B tests.

To be honest, I really want you to forget about the button color test example. The truth is, you can A/B test virtually anything. You can run A/B tests to compare different flows and processes, test new elements on a screen, experiment with showing different layouts or functionality to different user groups, and so on. The only thing to keep in mind is that the more things you change at one time, the less easily you'll be able to measure why a certain solution performs better.

My advice is to focus on the structure first—what you built up in the Define stage. Most of the time, a better information architecture will bring more results than just making changes to the visual design.

For example, think about a landing page. It's more likely that coming up with better copy and better content arrangement will lead to better performance than just changing button colors and typography. Don't get me wrong; those things are important, and sometimes you need to test them as well, but always know the order of things. If the information architecture sucks, your page sucks.

Here are two things you can test on your landing page right now:

Headlines and heading elements

Landing pages have a specific goal—presenting something and getting the users to take action. If you don't understand what a landing page is about, you'll abandon it. A huge part of this is copy and content. Headings are visually prominent, and when users are scanning the pages, they usually run through the headings. That's why it's vital to get them right. Run A/B tests to refine the headings on the landing page. Experiment with different copy and even different positioning.

Run A/B tests on the headlines and heading elements of a landing page.

Images

A picture is worth... nah, I'm not going to tell you again. You should know this by now. Visual elements are like images or videos that are easily scannable and draw the attention of the users. So finding a better picture to illustrate your product or coming up with a better background image that explains what the product's about is worth testing out. You'd be surprised, but sometimes a less sexy but more relevant image can beat a beautiful stock photo. Again, images are content.

If they're not relevant, they're just decoration. Test out different illustrations, images, and background images. Test out the best position for them.

Here are two things you can test on your e-commerce site right now:

Checkout process

No matter what kind of e-commerce site you have, it's always worth testing the shopping cart and checkout pages. For example, you can test the process itself. How many steps do you need? How can you best arrange the order of the steps users have to take to buy something? Test the microcopy. Come up with better instructions, better placement of the buttons, and input fields. Experiment with asking for more and less information. Remember, it's always a good practice to ask for the minimum amount of information from the users. Test the shopping cart too. Come up with a better arrangement as well as better microcopy and test it out. Focusing on the checkout process will have a direct impact on your conversions.

Get the most out of the images on a landing page by A/B testing them. Test out illustrations, background images, product images, or videos.

Test forms

Forms and input fields are great fields for testing. The more straightforward an input field is, the less likely your visitors will get confused and abandon the site. Test out placeholders and labels for the input fields. Come up with better microcopy for these. Test the success and error messages. A great error message will lead the users and can put them back on track again. Test out the arrangement of the form. For example, it's good practice to design a single column form, but sometimes you can bypass this practice. The goal is to be as straightforward and simple as possible for the users.

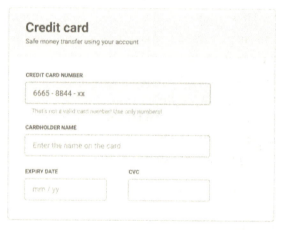

Test forms and input fields. Focus on labels, placeholders, and success and error messages.

Here are two things you can test on your mobile app right now:

Try different screen layouts.

Since you have very limited space on a mobile screen, it's worthwhile to experiment with different layouts. You have to make sure users can see the most important content and can access the most important functionality with ease. Create variations to optimize the navigation. Experiment with different layouts for the same screen.

Do A/B tests to refine the layout of your mobile app.

Optimize your store's appearance.

If you've ever downloaded an app, you know that you only see the icon and title of the app with some screenshots and a few lines of description before you download it. As a user, you have to make a decision to buy and download a specific app based on this information. With that said, your appearance in the app store can be a deal maker or a deal breaker. Therefore, it's best to run A/B tests. You can test the icon of the app. This is the first visual element users are going to see. If you need to, come up with better screenshots, videos, and designs when displaying what your app can do. Then, run A/B tests to find the best screenshots, best description, and best title for the app to get the most out of your app installs.

Optimize your store's appearance with A/B tests. You can reach more visitors and get more downloads by optimizing the images and text that appear on your store page.

Do A/B tests!

Set your goals.

The first step is to set goals for the tests. They can be to increase conversions or to decrease the churn rate of the shopping cart page.

Analyze the product and generate test hypotheses.

With your goals in mind, take a closer look at the product and hunt for problems. What could you improve to boost the performance of the product? What issues are users facing? Use analytics and do usability tests. Analytics will tell you "where" the problems are. Usability tests will show you what users are thinking and what challenges them in your product. The goal is to get as many ideas as possible on what to test out in the product.

Sort your test hypotheses.

Once you get into it, you'll have a lot of different ideas. There will be ones that can be tested out right away and others that will take a bit more thinking. Craig Sullivan, conversion specialist, created a great method for organizing test hypotheses. The only thing you have to do is to decide which of your ideas go into which bucket:

Bucket	Description	Example
Things to implement	Don't need to test because it's obvious it's going to improve the product. All you need to do is implement and measure.	The text size is too small and hard to read. Just make it bigger.
Measure better	You don't have enough information about this question because currently you are not measuring it. You need to collect data first.	You need to measure the clicks on the shopping cart button to evaluate if it performs well or not.
Questions to investigate	You can see the problem, but you don't understand why the problem exists. You need to do more research to figure out the why.	You see a bad conversion rate when people are coming from mobile devices, but you don't know why.
Generate ideas	You can solve the problem multiple ways. You need to brainstorm multiple ideas that you can test.	Our goal is to make the visitors engage with our content and spend more time on the page. There can be a bunch of ways to support this goal.

Bucket	Description	Example
Go for a test	The problem is clear and you know how to solve it.	The copy of the hero section of the home page is confusing. We did interviews with users and now understand why it's confusing. We came up with a better version to test.

Decide what to test first.

When you have a backlog of things to test, you have to decide what to test first. A/B testing takes time and traffic, so prioritize wisely. Below, I'll show you a spreadsheet that will help you to prioritize test ideas. All you have to do is insert your ideas in the table and go through a bunch of questions for each of the ideas to score them. In the end, you'll have a score for each test idea so you can decide what to test first. Insert your ideas into the table, then answer the following questions:

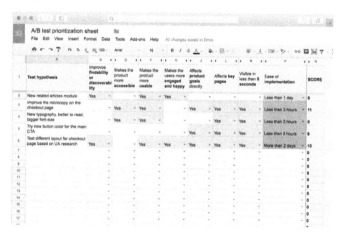

A/B Test Prioritization spreadsheet.

308

Is the idea improving the findability/discoverability of the product or a feature?

If we implement the idea in question, will it help users discover the product or feature easier, or will they find information faster inside the product?

Does the idea make the product more accessible or improve performance?

Accessibility and performance play a huge role in UX. Accessibility means that you can use the product with ease despite limited capabilities, and I don't mean focusing only on people with serious disabilities like blindness or deafness. If you can't use a website easily while holding your phone with one hand, that's an accessibility issue. Performance is also accessibility. If the page takes too much time to load, it's not easily accessible. Bugs, performance issues, and error handling are also crucial to the experience.

Does the idea make the product more usable?

Does this idea affect how usable the product is? Does it make it easier for users to use?

Does the idea make the users more engaged and happy?

It also counts if an idea has an impact on the engagement of the users. If they're happy and engaged, they'll spend more time using the product.

Does it affect product goals directly?

If a test idea has an impact on the product goals, it's a priority. For example, for an e-commerce site, improving the forms of the checkout page directly relates to the conversion rate. The better and more convenient the forms are, the more likely users will fill them in.

Does it affect key pages?

There are screens in a product that play an important role in the conversion funnel. If you plan to make changes to the landing page, exit page, checkout page, or payment page, then that's a priority.

Is it visible within five seconds?
If something is visible within five seconds, it means most users will see it. If you plan to change something that falls into this category, it's best to test it out as early as possible.

Is it easy to implement?
Finally, you have to consider the amount of effort needed to implement a certain idea. Obviously, the less time it takes to implement something, the higher it scores. Adding ease of implementation information will give you a complete picture of which idea will have a huge impact on the experience and won't take much time to develop. That's the one to test first.

Create variations and set up the test.
Next, you need a tool to create the tests themselves. Here's the software I recommend trying out:

Optimizely
This is one of the most recognized A/B testing tools out there. Optimizely offers a wide range of tools for website personalization, analytics, and mobile testing.

Visual Website Optimizer (VWO)
VWO was created for marketers without IT support. It's a simple platform that allows you to create an A/B test and get visual feedback on the designs (like heatmaps).

Unbounce
Unbounce focuses on landing pages. They offer a tool to create landing pages from templates and A/B test them. The benefit of this tool is that

you don't need developers and engineering to create a simple landing page for you; you can do it on your own with Unbounce.

Run the experiment and analyze the results.
After you set up the test, you can sit back and wait for the results to come in. There's only one challenge for you at this stage: Don't stop the test too early! Don't stop until the data is solid! Otherwise, all your efforts will be wasted. When the test is finished, the tool shows you the winning version and conversion rates. It also tells you if the results are significant.

There are three cases:

- The variation beat the original version and it was significant. In this case, you can be 95% sure that the variation is better.
- There's no significant difference between the variations. This is the most common result. The variation might be a little better, but it's hard to tell.
- The original version beats the variation.

In the first case, we can be happy. We solved the problem and can be almost sure that if we implement the winning variation, it will improve our product.

In the second and third cases, you have to investigate what could have gone wrong. Look through the following possibilities:

There was a technical issue with the test.
First, check that you didn't screw up anything in the tool.

The hypothesis is good, but your solution sucks.
It can happen that you saw the real problem and tried to fix it, but users just didn't like the solution you came up with. So, you won't see a signif-

icant result. If this happens, come up with a better solution. Do some research; do usability tests or interviews to understand what the problem is with your solution and start over.

<u>You didn't segment the users.</u>
It's possible that not all your users experience the problem that you're trying to solve. Some users are affected by the issue, and they're happy with the solution. But others aren't concerned. If all the users are involved, the test might not be significant. In this case, you have to segment the users and only run A/B tests with the potential users. You can segment users based on the traffic source, behavior, or the device they're using.

Implement the winning variation and start over.
The final step is to implement the winning variation and move on to the next test. A lot of people think of A/B tests as the last trial an idea has to withstand. The only problem with this approach is that if you fail, you'll be disappointed. And chances are, you will fail at first.

Instead, think of A/B tests as steps that take you toward completing your goals. It takes a lot of steps to get there. Sometimes you'll take one step, sometimes three, and sometimes you have to back up a few steps. The point is, the more testing you do, the further you'll go.

Key takeaways

- Validating the designs and the product is an essential part of UX.
- Pay attention to first-time user experience; make sure you don't lose visitors due to a bad first impression.
- Five-second tests are viable tools for understanding the first impressions of the user. Use five-second tests to fine tune your landing pages, branding, and messaging.
- Click-tests are a micro-usability test. Use click-tests to test out the vital interactions on your site, such as call-to-action buttons.
- Doing usability tests will show you the strengths and the weaknesses of a product. You'll see where users get lost, what they find difficult to use in your product, and how engaging the product is for them.
- Usability tests can be done in various ways: in person, remotely, moderated, and unmoderated. The best thing to do is to stick with in-person tests whenever you can. But if your budget is tight or you're behind schedule, unmoderated tests can bring invaluable insights as well.
- Use A/B tests to test different versions of a design. A/B tests can show you if one design performs better than another. Learning A/B testing takes time and practice. Don't think that it's an easy path. It's just as difficult as any other research or analytics.
- If you don't have traffic for A/B tests, do other tests instead. You can run multiple five-second tests and click-tests at the same time, then fine tune your designs in a fraction of the time that A/B tests take.

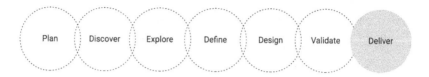

#7 Deliver

Design Handoff

This is the end of the process. Well, sort of. When you've validated the visual designs, the next step is the development. This is when developers start working with the designs and the product starts taking shape. We already discussed the importance of involving developers in the UX process; they can add a lot of value since they're closely focused on the technical execution and constraints. This is helpful because they've already provided feedback and know how the product works before they start working with the designs.

Create the design handoff documents.

Preparing the designs for developers and handing off the work is often an overlooked and pain in the ass part of the process. If the designers aren't thorough and don't prepare everything the developers need, the difficulties will begin. In most companies, designers send Sketch files, PSDs, or worse, Illustrator files to the developers, wishing them good luck. This is like trying to teach your son how to cook scrambled eggs by just giving him a pan and some eggs. At the Deliver stage, you have to be careful and do everything you can to help the developers with their work.

314

- By only seeing the designs, it might not be clear to developers how the product works. If it's not clear, they'll start bombarding you with questions.
- If you're working with lots of screens, it can hard for the developers to understand how they're connected.
- Developers have to break the designs down and slice images to begin their work. This could be a pain in the ass for them. Moreover, exporting the images in the right format and optimizing the file size is essential. This is easier and will save time if it's done by the designers.

Neglecting to dedicate attention to handing materials over to developers and supporting them in their work is bad for everyone. It's bad for the developers because they don't have everything ready for them, so they have to ask for the information. It's bad for the designers because they should be moving on to another design, but their time is taken up by questions and requests from the developers. It's bad for product managers because time is ticking away.

How to create a good hand-off

You have to understand how developers work and what they need for their work. Here's some no-brainer advice for you: Ask the developers what they need. This is so obvious, but it seems like everyone keeps forgetting about it.

I've worked with many different developers, companies, and in-house teams. Most of the time they needed the same things. However, they sometimes have unique requests. For example, there are developers who prefer to have a brief or specification for the designs as well as prototypes and all the design docs. Most developers I've met were happy to have the designers prepare all the images cropped and optimized for them, but there have been a few who preferred to do it on their own. Since we want to make developers happy and eager to work, it's vital to understand what they need for their work.

You need to hand these five things off to developers:

- Visual designs
- Design assets
- Prototypes
- Interactions
- Microcopy

I would like to add two extras that can skyrocket the developers' experience. A new trend is coming—developer experience. Anyway, here they are:

- Bonus #1: Hi-fi prototypes
- Bonus #2: Specification

Hand off visual designs and assets.

The first step in the development is the so-called front-end work. It involves breaking down the designs, cutting out image slices, and building up the designs in a format that a browser or mobile phone understands. Then, developers add functionalities like how a button should behave and what screen to show when the user fills in a form.

The front-end part of the development is similar to the designer's job. You need to slice images from the designs, format text, play around with typography, and measure the distance between the elements so that the working product will be as close to the designs as possible. That's why there are more and more designers learning to code and companies searching for visual designers with front-end development skills. I'm not saying the designer and front-end developer needs to be the same person. But I am saying that you need a strong collaboration between developers and designers to ensure the best quality. Likewise, front-end developers have to understand design principles and have a good eye for design. This is especially true because they're the ones who have to build what the designers have designed.

That being said, you need to send the designs to the developers. Shall we just send them the Photoshop or Sketch files then? Absolutely not. Design software like Sketch and Photoshop are made for design work, not for front-end work (but if one of them must be used, Sketch is far better in supporting developers). Don't get me wrong; a developer can work with Photoshop files, but there are other tools that are made specifically for this purpose, and they save a lot of time and headaches.

Below are a few tools I recommend checking out:

Figma
Since Figma files are updated in real time, the handoff happens automatically. You just need to grant view-only access to developers, and there you go—they can see the designs, export assets, and start working. Figma also has a direct integration with Zeplin (see below), which is a tool actually built by developers for developers to make handoffs easier. A word of caution for all Figma fans out there: it's easy to get lazy because you don't need to send files and there's no need to prep assets. All you have to do is enter the developer's email address and the problem is solved. Exported assets from the designs can be a challenge for developers, so don't forget to offer your help and make sure they have everything they need.

Avocode

Avocode was among the first tools out there to help with communication and handoffs between designers and developers. You can upload Sketch and Photoshop files to the cloud, and developers can work with them without having to buy and install the design tools. They can export assets, see color codes, and copy and paste CSS styles. The best part is that it runs on the cloud, so a bigger team of developers and designers can work with the designs at the same time without disturbing each other.

Zeplin

Similar to the above two, Zeplin is also a collaboration tool for designers and developers. As a designer, you can easily upload all of your Sketch files or PSDs and add colors, styles, and comments. Zeplin even creates a style guide for you. As a developer, you get all the information you need to start working—you can see the designs, download image slices, view the designer's comments, see colors, download fonts, and much more.

InVision inspect

If you're using InVision already, I have good news for you. InVision added a new feature called "Inspect," which does almost the exact same thing as the above tools, but it does it inside the tool you're already using. You can measure the distance between elements, export assets, and copy CSS the same way. A big advantage is that you don't need another tool; your team can use InVision through the whole process.

No matter what solution you choose, the goal is to show the designs to developers in a form they can work with. They don't need to work inside a design tool. What they need is a flexible environment where they can measure the distance between elements and easily get the styling information to write the CSS code. You'll also have to prepare image slices, fonts, and any other content that they need during their work.

When handing materials off to developers, run through this checklist:

- All the designs have been prepped for the developers (exported in an easily digestible format or using a solution like Zeplin).
- All the fonts used in the design are prepared.
- Image slices are prepared in the appropriate format (SVG, PNG, JPG).
- Content is prepared (microcopy, copy, video, etc.).
- The style guide is prepared (if there is onethere's any).

Prototypes and microcopy

Now the developers have all the designs with all the assets prepared. Good job! But they need to see how the screens relate to one another. They have to understand how the product works. We need to show them the interactions.

If you have followed the *7STEPUX®* process, you'll have prototypes for the visual design. Great! Now it's time to share them with the developers. Since they're clickable, the developers can try them out and see the whole product in action. If you're dealing with a bigger project, you'll probably have multiple prototypes (e.g., separate prototypes for the desktop and mobile version). It's best to list the prototypes in a document and explain which prototype shows what.

Use Tour Points in InVision.

Sometimes you need to add a bit more of an explanation to the designs in order to be straightforward. If you're using InVision, check out Tour Points. Add your comments on the screens—but instead of regular comments, choose to add Tour Points. As a result, when somebody opens up the prototype, they'll be able to go through the comments one by one and navigate between them. It's like an onboarding with tooltips where you're walked through the screens.

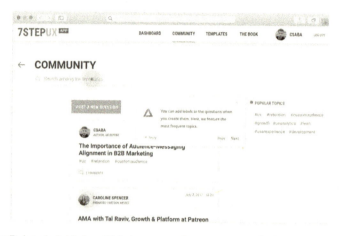

Tour Points in InVision. This is an excellent way to walk the developers and other team members through the designs.

Microcopy

Always pay extra attention to the microcopy. Developers can see and copy the microcopy from the designs, but the designs usually don't show 100% of the microcopies. As a designer, you don't usually create new designs just to showcase the success and error messages. Buttons can have different states, and their labels can also change. For example, a cart button has a different copy when empty than when you add something to the cart or when you have an abandoned cart. It would be a waste of time and huge overhead to create separate designs just to show that there's a change in the copy.

You need a good way to document and list out all the microcopies. The best way to do this is to create a spreadsheet for them. I prefer to use a cloud-based solution like Google Spreadsheet because it's easy to share and collaborate with your team.

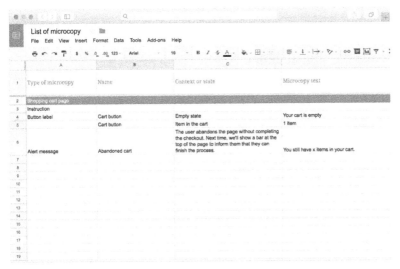

A spreadsheet that lists all the microcopies. A simple way to keep track of every instruction, button label, and error and success message.

Start adding the microcopy information into the spreadsheet.

- Specify the type of copy (e.g., instruction, button label, and/or success or error message).
- Specify the location of the copy (e.g., checkout page).
- Specify the context or state (e.g., button hover).
- Input the microcopy text.

Having this list of all the microcopies will help you keep track of them so you're not only focused on the visible texts.

Bonus #1: Hi-fidelity prototypes

We talked about hi-fidelity prototypes in the Design chapter. These prototypes are great to show how a complex animation or interaction should behave. When you create one, it's worth sharing it with developers.

Bonus #2: Specification

Most of the time, the prototypes with the assets, design brief, and other materials are enough for developers to start working. However, some developers prefer to have a document that describes how the screens are connected together, how each function works, and so on. Since it's your job to prepare everything for them, make sure you first ask them what they need. Show the prototypes and all the other assets, then let them decide whether they need a specification as well.

Look in your own backyard

We talked about handing over the designs to developers. However, it's also vital for designers to have the designs in an organized and clean manner. Creating the product design is not a do it once project but rather a continuous piece of work. Designers will continue working on new features, improving the product, and contributing to the new releases of the product. Therefore, you need to organize the design files and constantly update the design system so that the designs don't become obsolete and behind the actual product.

Developers hate to work with messy code. Likewise, as a designer, don't waste your time staring at chaotic design files. Home.psd, Home1.psd, Home-1-final.psd—sound familiar? If so, you know you're in trouble.

Every designer in this world

It's funny because it's true. But it shouldn't be.

So, dear designer, when you prepare materials for developers, make sure all the design files are updated, synced, and named intuitively—and have them organized. Think ahead! Imagine that you have to work on a particular file after a few months have passed. Could you still use it with ease? Here are a few tips that only take a minute to do for each design file, but will save you from a lot of headaches in the long term:

Don't delete; archive!

Nowadays, we rarely face storage issues. Cloud storage is cheap, and so is an external drive. It's risky to delete a design file during the process. You never know if you'll need that design in the future. But if you don't delete duplications and unnecessary design files, your folders will quickly get cluttered.

Instead of deleting, create an "Archive" folder. Put the duplicated files, experiments, and unnecessary designs in that folder. Then, after a while, start deleting the old, obsolete files from that folder to free up storage on your drive.

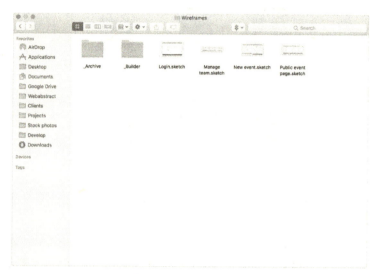

Create an "_Archive" folder for the design files you don't need. This is an easy way to keep your folders organized, and you avoid the risk of losing important files.

Don't forget to do the same thing with web-based tools like Figma! Without keeping the layers, files, and components organized, the chaos will quickly spread. I like to add an "Archive" page to every Figma file I'm working with and send every frame and design asset to it that I don't need at the moment. It's not taking up storage space, so why delete it?

Keep your design files clean.

Whether you're using Figma, Sketch, Photoshop, or other tools for creating the visual designs, you have to keep your files in order.

- Delete unnecessary and unused layers.
- Group the layers so it's easier to navigate.
- Add intuitive names for the layers. Trust me, you'll thank me for this later on. No more "Layer Copy 23," please!
- Delete unused artboards (if you're using Sketch, you can create an "_Archive" page to store the artboards and design elements you don't need).

Always leave a tidy workspace—not just in the real world, but digitally speaking too. Trust me, it feels so much more professional to have a clean working environment as opposed to a messy desktop that you're embarrassed about when sharing your screen and showing your work to clients. Sound familiar? Don't wait until it adds up. Do it now!

QA during development

The next thing in the process is to start developing the working product. This is when developers come in. It's very important that designers and developers collaborate on the working product. There are a lot of minor details that are not featured in the designs. No matter how high-fidelity you go with your prototypes, they're still not the final product. This is why it's extremely important to have a good quality assurance process during development. The designers have to make sure that the designs are implemented in the right way. Here are a few tips to get the best results:

When a part of the product is ready, review it with the designers.
When the developers finish parts of the product, the designers have to have time to sit down and review it. This shouldn't be a pain in the ass; it should be an activity that ensures that the designs are implemented correctly. If you're working in an agile environment, it's even easier. You just have to dedicate time to review after each sprint.

When you've finished a part, sit down with the designers and do the following:

- Make sure that the designs were implemented in the correct way and that everything is in place.
- See if anything is missing (e.g., a hover state or something you didn't think of before).

Dedicate time for fine tuning.
The *7STEPUX®* process uses a smart and detail orientated design process. However, you have to accept the fact that no matter how hard you try, there will always be things to improve on in the designs when developers start working. There will be things that you only realize when you see the working product. Therefore, you have to dedicate time for fine tuning. This means that designers and developers take the time to sit down together and make changes to the product. And, often, it means that designers have to change a few things in the designs as well in order to make it outstanding.

Do a Design Review.
Use the Design Review exercise that we covered in the Define chapter—it's not only for designs but also for the working product. Invite the developers, designers, and researchers to participate in the activity and review the finished parts of the product.

End of the process... Or is it?

This is the entire process of designing a product and applying smart UX design. However, this shouldn't be the end of the design. This is when the hard work begins.

Most companies put most of their efforts into creating the first version of a product—even companies who work with UX designers. The funny thing about this is that product development is about iteration—continuously creating a better version of the product. You don't design the "final," full-blown dream product. Instead, you go step by step to continuously build the product that serves your business and users' needs.

Think about a staircase (again)! Most companies are standing in front of the stairs, summoning all their energy and trying to jump over as many stairs as possible at once. Maybe they can jump three or four steps at once, especially those who put focus on UX and applied research. But all these companies are doing is trying to create the best first version possible. Then, they most likely run out of time and money, and the development of the product slows down. And this is after they go to the market! It's insane! It's even worse when, despite all their efforts, the first version isn't that good.

Instead, go step by step. Go for a minimum version of the product. Throw out everything that's not extremely important to have in the first version. Ask yourself this question for every feature: Can I go to market without having this feature?

Going step by step means you go to market earlier and start getting feedback from your actual, paying users. This means you'll save a lot of time and money by not wasting your efforts on creating something that's most likely going to end up being changed anyway.

Instead of a do-it-once project, work on the UX continuously. This way, you can learn from the market feedback and start building a better product. It's not the first usability test or the first A/B test that will bring success. Success begins when your users are happy with your product, love to use it, and look forward to new releases.

Success starts with knowing who your users are and having a great way to get their feedback to implement improvements into your product.

Iterate and start over!

This is the end of the process... Well, it's actually the beginning. Now we have to measure the success of the product, find out how to improve it, and go back to design and development. We have to go back to the user and business goals and research and testing. Only one thing has changed: You have a better product.

Start Now!

Start implementing UX step by step.

I frequently meet product managers and CEOs who are really into UX as well as data-informed thinking. They read all the books and blogs and follow the best practices. Still, it's difficult for them to figure out how to start implementing UX in their company. The theory isn't enough. That's why, in this book, I have given you a step by step solution and a process that you can follow in practice. However, I know it may still seem like too big of a bite to chew.

It's especially hard to bring a user-centered point of view into a larger, more established corporation. You need to rethink and change the process you use for product development. You need to hire new people and rearrange your teams. That's why there are more UX designers in the startup industry.

But let's be clear on one thing—UX and the *7STEPUX®* process is not a do-it or leave-it thing. I've taught you a process and lots of techniques in this book. By applying pieces of it, you can improve the products you are creating. For example, mapping out your business goals and creating your personas isn't a big step for you, but it's a huge step for your company when it comes to building better products.

My advice is to go step by step when introducing UX to your team and the company. The goal is that everyone feels comfortable enough to start thinking about business goals and user needs.

The goal is to replace the decisions made by a few executives with product decisions based on user feedback and measurement.

Start with a usability test!

One of the cornerstones of UX work is that it focuses on user needs. Therefore, a simple way to get started is to conduct a usability test. This won't cost you a lot of energy or money, and by doing so, you can show something actionable and useful. This will allow the whole team and company to see the power of involving users in the process. Do a usability test and meet your real-life users. If you follow the steps and guidelines I taught you in the Validate chapter, you'll end up having practical but easy to implement feedback from the test. This is extremely important. You have to show yourself and the company that this is not some obscure science; it's something that can help you build a better product right here, right now.

If you can only do one thing, do a usability test. By introducing usability tests you'll give a boost to your projects. Share your experience with the team, and involve others in the tests. Show your company that you're building a product for real people and that you can use their feedback to build a better product.

Expert advice

When doing a usability test, do a mini user interview with your users. Ask a few questions about their problems and how they're currently using the product in order to understand a bit more about how they think.

Start designing flows instead of screens.

Wireframing is important, but it's not wireframes that make a better and smarter design process. I'm not saying you shouldn't start doing wireframes. I'm saying that before you do, start thinking about flows and stories instead of screens. Every function in a product is a story. Behind every function, there are user needs and goals as well as context (where, when, and how will the users use it). You need to think of these first. Try storyboarding, draw task flows, and write out users' stories for your product. By applying flow-based thinking, you can avoid dead ends. You'll also create better and smarter designs.

Make it a group activity.

UX is highly collaborative; it's not a one-man-show to create a design for an app or website. Good UXers will help the product team brainstorm better, design better, develop better, and focus on the business and user needs better.

Start by introducing the Design Studio exercise to brainstorm solutions to a design problem. This makes the design a thing the whole team will think about (not just the designers). Start doing Design Reviews to review the finished designs and developed parts of the product. This will help you get more quality feedback for the product.

The whole point of collaboration is to speed up the feedback loop. For example, the later you show the designs to developers, the more risk you take by bypassing the technological constraints. If you don't include stakeholders in the project planning, you won't have a clear focus and scope of the project.

It's not difficult to take these three steps, but if you had already taken them, you would have a solid UX foundation in your company. You can even take the steps one at a time. Later, you can add more from the *7STEPUX®* and the process as a whole. Apply more research from the Discover chapter to get the most out of project planning and apply a smarter design process following the Explore-Define-Design chapters. The more you apply it, the better results you'll see.

Also, don't get lost in the weeds! The build-measure-learn doesn't work if you take out one of the steps. So don't waste your time finding the perfect way of prototyping or the best visual design until you've found a way of measuring and testing out your ideas.

Should you hire a UX agency or build an internal team?

I know that everything we've covered so far sounds great, but someone has to sit down and do it all, right? This immediately brings us to the question of whether you should build your own UX team or work together with a UX agency.

I've met lots of companies that knew it was time to invest in UX, but they only saw building an internal team as the path to success. However, this is a difficult path. To build up a great UX team, you have to hire the right people—and it's not enough to just get one UX designer. On the other hand, I've worked with a few companies that could have built their own UX team, which would have allowed them to iterate the product faster.

If you're about to make a decision, I'll help you out with a few tips and tricks here. Let's take a look at why it's good to build an internal team of designers and what the benefits of working with an agency are. One thing I won't touch on here is pricing. I know pricing is a crucial factor in making this decision, but it varies from country to country. You can look up how much it costs to hire a UX designer and also get quotes from decent agencies on your own. After you've done this homework, take a look at the pros and cons of each solution below.

Why is it good to work with a UX agency?

If you've never worked with UXers or don't have any of the competencies in-house, it's worth working with a UX agency first. A good UX agency will have a great process you can learn from. They've worked on various projects and can adapt to a particular business. This is extremely useful when starting out with UX. You can take their process, use their resources, and learn from their experience.

Unlike building a team, if you work with an agency, they can allocate as many resources as you need for the project right away. For a smaller project, you usually have a UX designer and a visual designer. For a larger project, it might be good to have a separate UX researcher as well, and grow the team as needed.

It's also a good idea to hire an agency if you're designing the first version of the product. Most of the time, it's cheaper to create an MVP (minimum viable product) with an agency compared to hiring people for that gig. Later, if the product is successful, you can build the product team around it step by step.

The very best thing about working with an agency is that they'll bring new and fresh ideas to the table. You can use their creativity and experience that has been battle-tested in many projects and many businesses.

Here are some tips for working with an agency:

- Find an agency that's focused on UX. A simple digital agency or design agency might not be the one you're looking for.
- Look for companies with relevant experience in your line of business. The agency you choose has to learn about your business and market. If they already have relevant experience in your market or a tangent market, you won't be starting from zero. For example, if I were to build an analytics tool or CRM, I would pick an agency that has experience in creating complex web applications.
- Visual design is important, but it's not what will make your product great. Don't pick the agency with the shiniest designs. Pick the one that focuses on users and the business side. Look especially for the business side. If an agency isn't interested in your business, you're already doomed.
- Pick an agency that's willing to work with your team and share their knowledge with you. Maybe they can also help you build your own team. The best UXers don't want to keep their knowledge to themselves. They love to teach and spread the UX word.
- Only work with people who involve you in the process. If they start organizing workshops and asking you to invite stakeholders and developers, you're on the right track. If they ask for a brief and start working, you know you're in trouble.
- Always make sure you meet and know the people you're working with. Some companies apply the bait-and-switch technique. This means they'll send their best, most senior colleague to the meeting to sell the service. Then, they pass the project along to a junior guy. Make sure you know the people you'll be working with. It's not a problem if they involve junior designers, but they have to be transparent about who will be working on the project.

Expert advice

Ask to do a full-day workshop with the agency you want to work with before diving into the project. Talk about your business, map out your users (start the Plan phase), and brainstorm. Good agencies will be happy to do this with you. This is a good opportunity for them to get to know you and showcase their talent.

Why is it good to build an internal team?

To do great UX, you need a great team. As I said, it's not a one-man show. You can't expect somebody to consider business goals, focus on user needs, design flows and screens, and do all the research and testing.

The best part of building an internal UX team is that you bring the UX competency in-house; it's no longer something that you "import" from an external company. Instead, the whole company can access the UX knowledge.

In-house UXers will know your product and users far better in the long term. They'll work with them more and follow all the iterations of the product. There are several techniques and activities that work better with an internal team (e.g., Design Studios, collaborative sketching, and Design Reviews). Just think about it. With an external team, it's not as easy to do a Design Studio or other workshop as it is in-house, where you just have to walk into the next room and invite a few colleagues.

Another point for team building is that you need UX in the long term. It's not worth applying UX to just one project or one product. That's like saying, "In this project, we're interested in user needs and in building a successful product. But in the next project, we don't care." I think that every company that builds digital products needs a good UX team.

Here are some tips for building a better UX team:

- If you're starting up, you need to hire senior people. The first step is to create the process and see how to fit UX into your company. For this, you need experienced UXers who understand the business and have experience in building a team and communicating UX values to the stakeholders.
- Find somebody who's interested in the business. As with agencies, you don't want somebody who's all about drawing wireframes.
- Continuously build the team. After you get UX designers and visual designers, hire a dedicated UX researcher. Then, open a position for content strategy.
- Don't limit UX to design only. Product decisions are business decisions. Deciding which features to put in the product shouldn't come from top management; this should come from knowing the business goals and understanding the user needs.
- Build a UX-friendly environment. The path to success is when everyone on the team and in the company "owns" UX and loves to think in a design-centered way.

Get the best of both: Build an internal team and work with agencies

If you want the best results, you should do both. Work with a UX agency if you're starting out. Use their experience and their resources and learn their process. This way you'll jump-start the process and see results faster. If you already have designers (e.g., visual designers), involve them in the process. You can also ask the agency to tutor your colleagues. If you already have a UX team or UXers, you can use the agency's resources to build the product faster.

Meanwhile, use all these resources to build your own team. In the long term, you'll need dedicated people working on your product (once you're an established business). They'll know the product, your business, and your users better than any agency. But, an agency can help you get started. Hire a senior UXer who will work well with the agency. It will be a huge help for the senior colleague to use the agency's resources while they dig deeper into the business and build up the processes for the company.

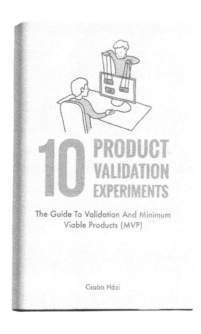

The Guide To Validation And Minimum
Viable Products (MVP)

Csabo Házi

Your Guide To Validation: Introducing The 10 Product Validation Experiments

Product validation experiments (PVEs) are tools used to validate product/service ideas. If you've heard "MVP" before, you might feel a little confused right about now. Aren't they the same thing? Ideally, an MVP (minimum viable product) only features the must-have functionality of the product, and you only invest the time and money that's absolutely required to create that first version, nothing more. On the other hand, a PVE has only one objective—to test if a business idea will fly using whatever validation technique necessary. The difference between an MVP and a PVE is that the MVP is scalable. The MVP is the first version of your product——a bare-boned, essential version.

The PVE is an experiment that you can use to test an idea WITHOUT actually building the product. If you want to build a mobile application, creating the first version of the app is not a PVE. That would be your MVP. But creating a video showcasing what the app could do and putting that on a website is a good example of a PVE.

Originally, product validation experiments were part of this *7STEPUX®* book. You might be thinking, "Hey, wait a second, I know what you're doing! You're just doing this to sell more books!" Well, yes and no. Although I love the idea of selling more books, it's more about separating validation from the process of designing and building a product. The *7STEPUX®* process will help you design a kick-ass product, while Product Validation Experiments will teach you tactics you can use to quickly test out a product or business idea before you actually build it.

In my Product Validation Experiments book, I cover 10 specific validation techniques with lots of case studies and stories from smart entrepreneurs. Tactics discussed include

- Fake Door Testing
- Wizard of Oz
- Concierge Service
- Product Video
- Landing Page Validation
- Crowdfunding
- Pre-order
- Piecemeal Product
- Concept Prototype
- Webinar

Maybe you're already familiar with some (or most) of these tactics, but don't close this book just yet! Before you assume this is just another general book with the same few well-known examples you read in every other article about MVPs and validation, let me tell you why I wrote it. I was fed up reading the same examples over and over. I remember reading about the concepts the first time, and it hooked me immediately. The stories about successful examples for validation (Dropbox, Zappos, etc.) sparked my imagination right away. But I was stuck with some questions: How do I get started? How do I adopt these awesome concepts to my own business ideas? I started researching and, at that point, it turned out that everyone was just using the same stories and the same examples were circling around on the internet.

Fast forward a couple of years, and with several projects behind me, I decided to solve this problem and go above and beyond by collecting as many great and detailed case studies from my own experience and from other smart entrepreneurs I trust and turning it all into a book format. That's why this book isn't just a collection of well-known stories. It's an in-depth investigation of each validation technique so that you can adapt them to your own business.

For each experiment, I teach you when to use it and what pitfalls to look for; I also give you plenty of stories to spark your creativity.

I recommend this book to any entrepreneur who wants to build digital products. It will save you plenty of time and money by helping you validate your business or product idea, and it will help you avoid building a business that won't fly.

Sound exciting? Get your hands on a copy by following this link:

csabahazi.com/10PVE

Thank You

Before we wrap things up, I want to say thank you for purchasing my book. I know you could have picked so many other books on UX and product design, yet you chose this one. I hope you enjoyed it and that it will serve you well as a handbook to a smart UX process.

You might think the author of a book gets a ton of feedback—reviews, emails with questions, and people reaching out all the time. At least that's what I used to think. In reality, like so many people, I used to read a book, and even if I loved it, even if it changed my life and helped me grow my business or helped me learn new skills, I just put it on the shelf without leaving a review or reaching out to the author to let them know they did a great job.

Don't get me wrong; I'm not here to complain. I just want you to know that I'm interested in hearing your thoughts. Did you like this book? Did you not like this book? I read every single review I receive for my books, and I treasure all the feedback I get when people reach out to me directly. And, guess what, I'm a human! I want to know if I did a good job or not.

Having said that, I have a little favor to ask of you. If you liked this book and you think other people might benefit from reading it, please leave an honest review on Amazon. I'm only interested in your honest feedback, and I promise I'm going to read it! Beyond feedback, reviews help me get this book in front of more people. The more reviews I have, the more Amazon and other platforms will think my book is a good read, so it gets more visibility on the platforms, and that translates into more readers.

Needless to say, if I get tons of negative reviews and everyone hates my books, I'm just going to stop writing them.

Please take a moment to follow this link and leave your review:

csabahazi.com/7STEPUX-review

About The Author

Csaba Házi is a product designer, an author, and a true entrepreneur by nature. He's constantly looking for new business ideas and problems to solve. He built up a successful UX agency in Budapest, Hungary, and has since joined the Toptal network, featuring the top 3% of elite freelancers in the world.

In 2017, Csaba published his first book on UX which became an Amazon Best Seller in the UX category. He has worked with dozens of startups and large international corporations but has always preferred to work with people who are making a real difference.

Csaba is very passionate about healthcare projects and education and is a frequent speaker at design and tech conferences.

It's dangerous to pitch a new business idea to Csaba——if it interests him, he'll try to figure everything out and design everything for you! He loves to answer questions and discuss new ideas, so feel free to reach out to him.

More on Csaba's work, books, and courses can be found at

csabahazi.com

www.ingramcontent.com/pod-product-compliance
Lightning Source LLC
Chambersburg PA
CBHW031236050326
40690CB00007B/820